Language Games and Activities

Simon Greenall

Hulton

Acknowledgements

I would like to thank Bernard Hoepffner and the members of 'Meeting Point – Lyon 2' at the University of Lyon 2 who helped me try out and develop many of these activities.

I am also grateful to Diana Pye, Pat Pringle and Heather Rea whose teaching inspired this book and who contributed a number of the activities.

Thanks are also due to Louise Aylward for her extremely useful comments, to Ron Hawkins and to H. A. Swan for encouraging me to write this book.

First published in Great Britain 1984
by Hulton Educational Publications Ltd
Raans Road, Amersham, Bucks HP6 6JJ

© Simon Greenall 1984

ISBN 0 7175 1272 X

Phototypeset by Input Typesetting Ltd, London
Printed in Great Britain by
Richard Clay (The Chaucer Press) Ltd, Bungay, Suffolk

Contents

Introduction

Drama, role-play, simulations, games – for some time, these terms have been as much part of the foreign language teacher's vocabulary as reading, writing, speaking and listening. All of these techniques are commonly used in the classroom to allow the students to practise the language they are learning. We also talk of 'warm-up' activities, 'improvisation' techniques, 'interaction' and so on – all words which seem to belong more to workshop sessions at a theatre school than to a foreign language classroom! So what do all these terms mean? And when should these kinds of activities be used?

Language Games and Activities is a book for teachers who are interested in giving lively and motivating lessons, and in creating the opportunity for spontaneous, authentic language practice in the classroom. It contains a number of ideas for games and activities which are all grouped together under themes, – People, Jobs, Travel, Shopping etc. – and which include indications as to the level at which they can be used, the language functions and structures which occur in them, the material and preparation required, and the time needed to complete them. They can be used as practice material to be integrated into conventional courses, or in situations where the group is of a less predictable nature in level and number, such as 'English Club' meetings which the participants attend in order to have an all-too-rare chance of speaking English, and which have to be fairly relaxed affairs. The activities are 'learner-centred' because the students are often asked to work in small groups, using their imagination and their own experiences to develop their own input material from an initial idea supplied by the teacher. For this reason, preparation time is usually minimal and very often involves no more than collecting together some source material or writing some words on a few cards.

But what is a language game or activity? What is the point of using them in a language class? And how exactly does the teacher organize them so that they can be performed as efficiently and profitably as possible? Before we look at the activities themselves, it will be useful to answer some of these questions.

What is a 'language activity'?

Clearly, every time the learner uses English either productively or receptively, s/he is involved in some kind of language activity. However, for the purposes of this book, the term 'language activity' is used to refer to any activity which is used to consolidate language already taught or acquired, and which occurs during the 'free' stage of a lesson or during occasions such as English Club meetings. Role-plays, simulations, improvisations etc. are all 'language activities'. The term 'game' is used whenever there is an element of competition between individual students or teams in a language activity.

Why use language activities?

In the classroom, the teacher and the course book exert a high degree of control over the language that students are learning by organizing it into manageable portions. Clearly it is essential that the students learn to manipulate the new input in the controlled conditions of the presentation and practice stages. But they must also start using the language meaningfully for themselves as soon as possible if they are to learn effectively. The language teacher has to encourage this transition to the production or free stage by simulating the real-life situations which occur outside the classroom.

Language activities are one way for the teacher to achieve this aim. In a language activity, students can produce meaningful and authentic utterances without the controlling influence of the teacher or the course book. At the same time, they are listening to language under simulated real-life conditions, with its natural qualities of repetition and hesitation, even if that language is at times contains errors of usage and grammar. Many learners express doubts about being exposed to the faulty language of their fellow students, particularly during the production stage. It might be true that the practice in the productive skill of speaking in these activities is more useful than the practice in the receptive skill of listening. But it nevertheless provides an occasion for learners to say 'I didn't hear' rather than 'I don't understand' when they miss certain information. More important – when students are learning English in non-English speaking countries, the only sources of authentic spoken language are the teacher's own speech (which is often stylized so as to be comprehensible to the students), radio broadcasts and recordings. In a language activity, whenever the learner is a listener, s/he is still hearing authentic language even if it is, at times, inaccurate.

Language activities are also useful to help the learning process. It is essential to maintain a careful balance between intensive practice and more relaxed work if the learners are to use their classroom time as efficiently as possible. Few students can concentrate for long periods without some change of pace, and even fewer will actually benefit from learning in such an intensive way in the long run. So calling some of these activities games should not detract from their serious nature and value as teaching techniques. However, it is equally important that the activities should not be a substitute for the more structured work of a well-organized course. An interesting activity will alter the pace of a lesson but will not replace the teacher's own measured presentation of the language to be taught.

The learning process is also helped by the simulation of need in the learners. Successful language learning has one important requirement: the students have to need the language before they will learn it. When they recognize that a structure or a word is useful to them, either immediately or in the future, they will be able to acquire it with the minimum of effort. Within the physical and conceptual limits of the classroom, it is not possible for the learners to recognize a need for all the language to which they are exposed, however useful they suspect it might be. So creating a simulated need through language activities is an effective aid to learning even if the need for the language is to win a game or solve a problem.

Language games and activities provide an opportunity for learners to try out their newly acquired competence in a context where they feel psychologically secure. They are less likely to be troubled by the fear of making mistakes since the consequences of inaccuracies and misunderstandings are fictitious and have no real significance. They are thus more likely to learn from their mistakes and can use these occasions to build up their confidence.

Later on in this book, the terms drama, role play, simulation etc. (see pp 11-12), are discussed. Many of these techniques would not seem out of place in drama school. Often a 'performance' of some kind is the focal point of the action. But this does not mean that the learners benefit only from the language used during the performance. The language used during the preparation before and the discussion afterwards is equally, if not more, important. Performance language is often scripted, at least mentally, and is likely to be less authentic and spontaneous than that used in preparation and discussion. Furthermore, the less polished the performance is, the more language it will generate, particularly in those activities such as mimes where the onlookers are asked to describe what they have seen.

So, why use language activities? Because they provide free and spontaneous practice of the language learnt in conditions lying half way between the controlled context of the formal lesson and the real-life situations outside the classroom.

The teacher's role

What do you, the teacher, do during these kind of activities? The answer obviously depends on the degree of control you choose to exert over the group. If the group is large, your conventional role of correcting and helping individual students is obviously limited. Similarly, if the activity is taking place during the warm-up or free stage of a class, it is better for the teacher to interfere as little as possible since the learners should be using this opportunity to experiment with what they have been learning. But this certainly does not mean that you can sit back and do nothing! As an illustration of how busy and useful you can be, here is a step-by-step guide to your role.

1 Your first task is to choose the activity. You may have a number of different criteria for your choice and the most obvious of these, structure/function, vocabulary, level of group, time available etc. are all indicated in each of the activities in the book. Many of the shorter activities are ideal for warm-up work at the beginning of a lesson which is often necessary, particularly when teaching abroad, to get the learners thinking in English again, perhaps for the first time since their last lesson. Be careful to leave yourself plenty of time for longer activities. It is a good idea to be prepared for an activity to finish five or six minutes earlier or later than you estimated. Don't forget that you can use these activities to practise or revise both vocabulary and functions/structures. If you decide to integrate one activity into a lesson because it practises the structure you are teaching at the time, try to choose or create one which revises what has been learnt during the previous lesson. You may also decide that you need to prepare the activity thoroughly, going through each stage of it in your mind. In this book, most of the ideas require little preparation, so that they can be used with groups of varying numbers. But if you know the size of the group, you can reduce the length of activities by preparing the input material yourself rather than asking the learners to do it. One last criterion of choice is that you should be prepared to do the activity yourself. You cannot ask the learners to do things which you would not or could not do yourself.

2 You then have to begin the activity. This sounds obvious but a certain amount of care has to be taken. If the activity is being used in a language club meeting, it would be clumsy to force the participants into action if they all seem to be happily engaged in conversation (in English, of course) with their neighbour and not just waiting for the proceedings to begin. Start when you feel that any natural conversation is beginning to die down, which usually happens after five or ten minutes. If you are using the activity as a warm-up, it can be an efficient and attractive way of starting work on time. In larger groups, attracting the attention of the participants can be a problem. The most efficient way is to clap your hands slowly, without speaking, until all the talking stops. This method preserves not only your dignity but also your voice for more important uses!

3 You then have to give instructions. These must be as simple and as brief as possible. With the more complicated activities, this is not always very straightforward. Remember that even after the most precise instructions, there will always be at least one group doing the opposite of what you have told them to do! First of all, if you want them to form groups, ask them to do so immediately. This reduces the inevitable confusion which momentarily reigns as an activity gets under way. Try to form small groups whenever possible; the smaller the group is, the more chance the participants have of speaking. Larger groups are more suitable when a participant has to perform a mime or describe something. The length of the activity can also vary according to the number and size of the groups; usually, the smaller the groups, the longer the

activity. Make sure that the stronger students do not always join the same group; it is important to have groups of mixed ability so that they can all finish on time. Then give a brief explanation of the setting and the ultimate aim of the activity. This must also be clear and precise, and you should use pictures, gestures and mime to convey this essential information. You will usually be able to tell quite quickly whether the participants have understood, but leave a short pause between each part of the instructions to let it sink in. It is effective both pedagogically and in terms of attractive presentation to use as few words as possible, and the careful preparation of this stage will help you avoid ambiguity and the consequent threat to the success of the activity. Similarly, the instructions should be followed by a brief example of part of the activity, only using, as far as possible, those words which the students are likely to use themselves. If the activity is complex, it is better to put the instructions on the board or to give new instructions before each stage in the development, since students find it difficult to retain a great deal of information and to perform the activity at the same time. Check that everyone has understood what has to be done and then let them get to work.

4 During the activity, go from group to group checking that they have understood and are carrying out the instructions. You will certainly be asked one or two questions about procedure, so make a quick visit to each group within the first two minutes. Then go round again, helping with vocabulary questions, correcting if you feel this is appropriate, giving encouragement and if necessary, inspiration for those games which require some imagination. It is always advisable to be ready with a few ideas on how *you* would carry out the activity. Many of the ideas in this book rely on the students reactivating vocabulary which has lain passive for some time, so encourage them to check with their partners before giving the words they need. If the groups are seated, you may like to make sure that there is a spare chair so you can join in with their work more comfortably, and at the same level as the students.

5 In discussion work, begin with small groups. These groups should then join their neighbours, report their conclusions so far, and then resume the discussion. This process should continue with each group doubling in size at each stage until you have two large groups representing the opinions of the whole class. This method creates a strong formal structure for the discussion. It is also easier to predict the total length of the proceedings and adjust if necessary.

6 When the groups are reaching the end of one stage of an activity, you must constantly check that they will all finish within a minute or so of each other. Nothing is more likely to lose the attention of a student than another group taking too long to complete its work. But if you have prepared the activity correctly by making sure the groups are not too different in level, they will all reach the end at more or less the same time. Announce in a loud voice how much time they have left at

regular intervals. Remember that it is better to draw proceedings to a close before inspiration and enthusiasm dries up, particularly in those activities which have no clear end.

Some activities will work better than others. Make sure that you have another idea ready to replace one which, for whatever reason, is not working. Students appreciate a teacher who recognizes that an activity is not right for the circumstances and abandons it quickly far more than a teacher who pushes on regardless.

Finally it is important to bear in mind that while you have only limited control over the *content* of the activity, you are in complete charge of the *form*. It is your responsibility to make sure that everyone has understood and can follow your instructions. You cannot hold the students entirely responsible if you suddenly discover that they are all doing completely different things. If this does happen, don't try and explain to each individual student; stop the whole class and give your instructions again.

Preparation

The majority of the activities and games in this book require little preparation. They do require, however, a carefully assembled stock of stationery and source material. You should obtain a large number of small cards, half the size of a postcard in at least four different colours, so that students playing different roles can identify each other by the colour of the card. If you cannot get cards in different colours, you can put crosses in different coloured ink on the backs of the cards. Alternatively, you can use pieces of paper cut to the suitable size. Larger pieces of card will also be useful for making clearly visible signs, as in the shop titles of 5.1. It is equally important to build up a library of source material. The following list will indicate the kind of material that can be used for language lessons in general, and the activities in this book in particular.

Newspapers
If you are working abroad, you might only buy an English newspaper every so often. Yet even a single copy can be used in a variety of ways. Make sure you keep interesting headlines, pictures and articles. Advertisements, the TV guide and crosswords can also be used.

Magazines
It is a good idea to buy colourful, well-produced magazines now and then for the pictures. Photography magazines are particularly useful for more creative and imaginative work, but ordinary 'Sunday colour'-type magazines are just as useful. Obviously if you are interested only in the pictures, it does not matter whether the magazine is in English or not. Some of the most stunning photography these days is to be

found in advertisements where often the language is as international as the product it is advertising.

Tourist and travel brochures
If you are abroad, it is possible that the nearest large town will have a tourist information service with regional brochures and town guides in English. Travel agents are a good source of free tourist literature.

Mail order catalogues
These are very useful if you want to build up a stock of vocabulary cards. You can cut out individual items of furniture and clothing etc., and stick them on to cards. Even whole pages can be used in activities such as 3.10.

Realia
Tickets, timetables, instructions, pamphlets, advertising handouts, postcards can all be used, particularly when doing narrative building, such as 6.4.

The preparation of these activities must also include the layout of the room you are working in. The worst kind of classroom is the one where there are desks fixed to the floor. In these conditions, you can only have the participants working in the empty area at the front of the room, or climbing over the desks. But if there are tables and chairs which can be moved, clear a large space in the centre of the room. Place the tables and chairs in small groups around the edge. Students seem to prefer this kind of arrangement to one where the chairs are simply pushed aside. Tables and chairs arranged like this encourage relaxed conversation. You will obviously want to stand and direct the proceedings from a point in the room where you will be most visible, e.g. by the board or OHP etc., so make sure that not too many chairs are facing the wrong way.

Techniques

Most of the games in this book are variations on a series of techniques. In many of them, it would be comparatively simple to change the vocabulary of the input material and create an activity that is better suited to your teaching purpose. Below is a list of the different techniques used in this book to help you invent your own games and activities. Remember that more than one can be used in the same activity.

1 Do-it-yourself simulation
A simulation is an activity in which the student plays him/herself in a situation which s/he has either experienced or can at least relate to in some way. In this book, the students are given separate cards with two

or three 'components' or different types of information (e.g. a situation, the name of a place, the name of a piece of furniture etc.).

The task is often a problem-solving activity where the outcome is successful if the participants use each of the components. The students themselves are often asked to create the components. For example, see 2.8., 3.6.

2 Role-play

This can be performed with jobs, famous people, characters or stereotype roles, particularly those to be found in the customer/service situation. The students are required to react in accordance with the identity or the role marked on the card, developing the character with improvised dialogue in either an everyday situation or a clearly defined setting. The first activity in this book is designed to get the students themselves to make role-cards which can be used for a variety of other activities. For examples of role-play, see 5.8, 6.6.

3 Describing

This is a simple situation in which one person has a certain item of information which s/he can only reveal by drawing, mime, roundabout description or Yes/no answers to questions put by the others. For examples, see 1.1, 3.1, 3.4.

4 Matching pairs

This is where words, pictures, lines of dialogue etc. are divided into two parts and then shuffled. One part is given to each of the students who must then find his/her partner using techniques described in 3. For examples, see 5.2, 7.2.

5 Jigsaw

This is similar to Matching pairs, but the word, picture etc. is divided into more than two parts. This is an effective way of teaching or revising words which are related in some way, such as ingredients in a recipe or items of furniture in specific rooms. Its most simple presentation is when pictures are cut up, shuffled and spread around the room. For examples, see 3.7, 4.8.

6 Logical sequences

This technique is similar to Jigsaw, but is used for material such as strip cartoons, song lyrics or proverbs of which the components (individual pictures, single words or sentences) can be reconstructed in the correct and logical order. When used with texts of various kinds, it can help the learner understand the importance of link words and sequencers. An odd-man-out can be introduced to make the task more difficult. It can also be used for more creative work where the students are given a number of components (words, pictures, objects) and are asked to organize them into their own logical sequence. This can give practice in narrative building. For examples, see 6.4, 7.8.

7 Boardgames

These take more time to prepare, but a lot of the work can be done by the students themselves. The simplest form is the snakes-and-ladders type where the players' progress along the course varies according to where they land on the board. You need to think of a situation which involves some sequence of events (e.g. a journey, a holiday, a shopping expedition) and then ask students to think of a number of favourable and unfavourable events which might occur as the players proceed. The game can then be laid out in either snakes-and-ladders or 'Monopoly' form. If the activity is too complicated, it may be necessary to put the instructions on the board. This is an extremely motivating technique. If the activity is done in small groups, it is a good idea to ask the students to pass the boardgame they have prepared to other groups. For examples, see 3.11, 6.11.

8 Discussion

Many of the activities can be used as a springboard for discussions or questionnaires. For examples, see 1.3, 2.10.

Sample presentation

Here is a detailed explanation of how to present an activity. It refers to 2.9 on page 32, but the organization and techniques can be applied to others in this book.

Setting

The activity is concerned with inventions and labour-saving devices, so begin by taking objects such as a pen, a key, a watch, sunglasses, a box of matches and asking students what they are used for. Ask students to think of an object and to describe it by saying what it is used for but without saying its name. If you already know your class, make sure you choose the more imaginative students. Encourage the others to guess the name of the object.

1 Point at the four nearest people to you and count in a loud voice '1-2-3-4'. Make a gesture with your arms outstretched as if you were pushing the group to the far corner of the room. Repeat the instruction two or three times to form other groups and wait until everyone has organized themselves into groups of three or four.

Take a card e.g. 'a device to squeeze the toothpaste tube flat'. Without speaking go to the board and draw a toothpaste tube. Ask students what you have drawn. Note that if you draw badly, you will elicit some amusing and varied responses. When they have guessed what you have drawn, draw a garden roller, or a hammer, or a weight marked 'One Ton' etc. Ask students what you have drawn. When they have guessed correctly, ask them what the connection between the two objects might be. If they have not guessed correctly after several suggestions, explain that you always have trouble in getting the last of the toothpaste out of the tube, and that you have decided to use a garden roller etc. to help you. Ask students if they have any other ideas.

Give a card to each of the groups, reading the card as you give it to them. Make sure that they understand the vocabulary. Return to the board and write instructions on how to use your device for getting the last of the toothpaste out of the tube. As you write, announce each instruction in a loud voice. Note that the instructions can be as humorous as you like: 'First, take the toothpaste tube into the garden. Next, open the garage doors and take out the garden roller. Then place the toothpaste tube on a hard surface . . .' When you have finished your instructions, make sure everyone understands that you do not think your device is very efficient. Then ask the groups to invent an efficient device to perform the task which is described on their cards.

As the groups start work, go round the class checking that everyone has understood what they have to do. Do this quickly and then return to any group which requires answers to more specific questions. Visit each group regularly checking that they are following your instructions. If more than two or three groups have not understood, stop the proceedings and explain again to the whole class. Be ready with a few ideas of your own to help the less imaginative groups. After ten or so minutes, check that all the groups are going to finish more or less at the same time. Announce how long they have to finish this stage of the activity.

2 When each group has finished, ask everyone to stop, and collect the cards. Take the toothpaste card again and read it aloud to the class. Ask one of the more lively students to stand beside you. Begin a dialogue: 'Every morning it's the same thing. I'm getting fed up with you, I really am . . . I'm tired of you going to the bathroom, taking the toothpaste tube and squeezing it from the middle. It really is too much. When I get to the bathroom, there's hardly any toothpaste left . . . etc.' Make it clear in your speech what the situation is and who the characters are. Encourage your assistant to make suitable responses. The success of this sample sketch depends on your ingenuity and the choice of assistant.

Give cards to each of the groups and ask them to prepare a sketch like the one you have just performed which illustrates why they might need the machine or device marked on the card. As the groups begin work, go round the class checking that everyone has understood what they have to do. Encourage them to write down notes rather than a complete script for the sketches. When the groups have nearly finished, announce how long they have to complete this stage of the activity.

3 When everyone has finished perform your sample sketch again with your assistant. Ask another student to describe the machine or device you invented in the first stage of the activity. Then point to one group and invite them to perform their sketch. When they have finished, ask the others to describe what they have seen.

Finally, ask the group which has designed a machine or device to solve the problem portrayed in the sketch to give their presentation. Repeat with other sketches.

You may like to attach the diagrams and instructions prepared by the groups on to the wall. If so, cut three pieces of paper into the shape of a rosette marked 1st prize, 2nd prize and 3rd prize. Ask the students to vote for the best three inventions and place the appropriate rosette by the diagrams and instructions.

Role card activity

The aim of this activity is for students to create the role cards which you can use in a variety of different activities in this book, such as 3.9. You will not necessarily need to do this activity each time you use role cards; you can try it out on one or two groups and keep the best role cards for future use. To a large extent, the role cards created here will be based on stereotypes. However, you may like to ask students to individualize them according to the particular activity by adding further information.

Language Describing impressions; describing personal appearance; giving opinions; agreeing, disagreeing

Vocabulary Physical appearance, clothing, housing

Level Intermediate   *Time* 20–25 minutes

Material Cards; a number of picture portraits of people. These should be as varied as possible e.g. a teenager, a student, a young businessman, a middle-aged couple, a manual worker, a housewife, an elderly couple etc.
A number of pictures of houses. Try and find examples of different kinds of houses e.g. a council house, a newly renovated flat, a cottage in the country, a bedsit, a penthouse flat, a large country house, a smart town house

Preparation None

---

1 Form groups of two or three. Give each group a picture of a person. Ask them to study the portrait for a few minutes and to build up an impression of the person, his/her lifestyle, what he/she does, where he/she lives, family and friends, leisure interests, education and even political views.

2 Spread the pictures of houses around the room. When everyone is ready, ask them to look at the houses and decide in which house the person in their picture might live. Each group should take a 'house' picture and continue to build up its impression of the person.
If two or more groups choose the same 'house' picture, they should justify their choice to each other and try to dissuade the other(s)

from choosing this picture. The other group(s) may then be obliged to choose a house which they feel is an unlikely residence for their person. However, encourage them to imagine the circumstances in which such a person would live in such a house; this will help them to create a more individualized role card.

3 When everyone is ready, ask each group to show the pictures they have chosen to the rest of the class, and briefly describe their person. Encourage the others to comment on the description and to contribute their own impressions.

4 Give each group a card and ask them to write down their impressions.

5 You may like to continue with an activity which uses role cards, or you may collect the cards and keep them for future use.

1 You and me
Talking about people

---

1 *Language* Asking questions

Vocabulary Non-specific

Level Elementary *Time* 15–20 minutes

Material Cards

Preparation None

---

1 Give a blank card to each student. Ask them to write down the name of a famous person e.g. Charlie Chaplin, Albert Einstein, Brigitte Bardot, Winston Churchill. Make sure that they do not show the card to anyone.

2 Collect the cards. Form pairs and give a card to one person in each pair.

3 **Variation 1**
Student B should ask Yes/No questions to discover Student A's identity. For higher level groups, you may like to impose a limit of twenty questions.

Variation 2
Student B imagines that he is in a situation (such as a railway carriage, at a bus stop) with student A with whom he starts a conversation. Student A should reply as her 'character' might reply in such a situation. Student B continues the conversation without asking any direct questions until he discovers student A's identity.

4 When student B has discovered student A's identity, give the former a different card and continue as in 3.

---

2 *Language* Present simple; present continuous; describing personal appearance

Vocabulary Clothing, physical appearance

Level Elementary *Time* 10–15 minutes

Material None

Preparation None

---

1 Form groups of five or six. Ask one member in each group to think of someone who may either be a well-known person or one of his/her fellow students. S/he should briefly prepare a description of this person's physical appearance.

2 **Variation 1**
The other members of the group should ask Yes/No questions about the physical appearance of this mystery person in order to guess his/her identity. You may like to impose a limit of twenty questions.

Variation 2
The student should give the description without mentioning the mystery person's name. The others are allowed to interrupt with questions.

3 The student who guesses the identity of the person being described continues as in 1 and 2.

---

3 *Language* Talking about likes, dislikes, preferences

Vocabulary Non-specific

Level Elementary   *Time* 25–30 minutes

Material None

Preparation Write the following on the board:

Food?	Spare time?	Music?	Politics?
Work?	Home life?	Books?	Family and friends?
Travel?	Cars?	Sport?	Education?

---

1 Form pairs. Explain that you are going to organize a series of questionnaires to find out more about the people in the class and to see which students will work well together. Ask each pair to prepare a questionnaire of ten or twelve questions using the themes marked on the board.

2 When everyone is ready, each pair should separate and each partner should try and question as many people as possible. Remind them to note down the name of the people interviewed and their replies.

3 After about fifteen minutes, the students should find their partners again and discuss the results. Ask them to decide which people have similar life-styles and interests. Would these people work well together in class?

4 Ask each pair to present its conclusions to the rest of the class. Encourage the others to agree or disagree with the views being expressed. Make sure they all use as many adjectives to describe people as possible.

4 *Language* Describing appearance and impressions; making deductions; giving reasons

Vocabulary Emotions, physical appearance

Level Elementary +   *Time* 15–20 minutes

Material Cartoons from newspapers or magazines; cards

Preparation Blank out any captions or dialogue in the cartoons

1 Form groups of three or four. Give a cartoon and a handful of blank cards to each group. Ask the students to think of adjectives to describe the appearance and the feelings of the characters in the cartoons. They should write each adjective on a separate card.

2 Collect the cards and shuffle. Collect the cartoons and redistribute to the groups. Give each group five 'description' adjectives. Explain that they must decide which of the five cards can be retained to describe the characters in their cartoons. Two students from each group should then look for other adjectives they need and get rid of any they don't need by going round the other groups and swapping cards. Explain that it is not necessary to find the five adjectives which were originally written down in 1 to describe their cartoon characters; they should merely look for adjectives which they consider appropriate.

3 The first group to find five adjectives which accurately describe the characters in its cartoon is the winner.

4 Spread the captions or dialogue that you cut off around the room. Each group should look for the captions or dialogue which belong to its cartoon, and check that it has chosen suitable description adjectives.

5 *Language* Present simple; present continuous

Vocabulary Non-specific

Level Elementary +   *Time* 25–30 minutes

Material Cards

Preparation None

1 Form groups of three or four. Number each group and give it a blank card. Ask its members to write down the name of a famous person (e.g. President of the USA, Queen of England, or a film star, a politician etc.).

2 Collect the cards, shuffle and redistribute, one to each group. Ask them to prepare a short mime sketch based on a day in the life of

the person on the card. Encourage them to include all the members of the group.

3 When everyone is ready, ask each group to perform its sketch to its neighbour (make sure this is not the group which wrote the card). If the group guesses the name of the person correctly, both groups win a point. If they do not guess correctly within four minutes, the group which wrote the card wins two points. You should keep score on the board.

4 Each mime sketch can be performed to all the groups except to the one which wrote the card. The winning group is the one with the highest score.

---

6 *Language* Describing impressions; describing personal appearance

Vocabulary Physical appearance

Level Elementary +   *Time* 20–25 minutes

Material Cards; Pictures of people in interesting, amusing or unpleasant situations. Photography magazines often provide a good source of this kind of pictures.

Preparation None

---

1 Give five blanks cards to each student. Ask him/her to write on separate cards five adjectives to describe physical appearance.

2 Collect the cards and shuffle. Make sure that there are not too many repetitions of the same adjective. Spread the cards around the room.

3 Form groups of three or four. Give each group a picture. Ask each group to discuss their impressions of the person(s) in the picture. They should write down eight or ten adjectives to describe these people.

4 The group should separate and go round the room looking for adjective cards which correspond with the words they have chosen to describe their picture. When the find the card, they should take it and place it beside their picture. Explain that if the adjectives which they thought of in 3 are not available, they should choose other suitable adjectives.

5 Ask one member of each group to stay by the group's picture, and the others to visit the other groups. Encourage students to discuss whether they agree or disagree with the choice of adjectives, using language such as: 'Why do you think she's cruel?' or 'I don't think he's very good-looking.'

6 Ask students to think about the lifestyles of the people in the pictures, what s/he does, where s/he lives etc. Encourage them to

discuss and justify their impressions of people judging them by their appearance. Do they make assumptions about people from the way they look and dress? What are the conventions concerning certain clothes for certain occasions? Do the students follow these conventions?

7 Give the students time to note down any words which they do not know. Then ask each group to think of situations in which the person(s) in its picture might have met those in the neighbouring group's picture.

---

7 *Language* Talking about plans and intentions; making predictions; giving advice

Vocabulary Non-specific

Level Intermediate   *Time* 25–30 minutes

Material Cards; twelve to fifteen horoscopes taken from different newspapers or magazines. These need not be all from the same day of publication.

Preparation None

---

1 Explain what a horoscope is and teach, if necessary the signs of the zodiac. Ask one student what she has got to do in the next few days, what arrangements to make, business matters and personal affairs to settle etc. Ask for the date of her birthday. Choose another student and ask him to read out the horoscope prediction for the first student's sign of the zodiac. Discuss with the others whether it is a good time for her to do all things she is planning to do.

2 Form pairs. Give each pair five or six cards and ask them to write on each one an important event in someone's life e.g. ask X to marry me, ask the boss for a rise, buy a new car, move to a desert island etc. Encourage them to think of events connected with work, family life, friends, romance, money etc.

3 Collect the cards and shuffle. Give five cards each to half the students. They must study them and try to adopt the identity of the person who has to do all these things. Give a horoscope to the other students. They should become astrologers.

4 The students with cards should find astrologers and ask them if they think it is the right moment to do all the things marked on the cards. The astrologers must consult the horoscope and give advice.

5 The students with cards may like to seek advice from other astrologers who have different horoscopes.

8 *Language* Non-specific

Vocabulary Non-specific

Level Intermediate   *Time* 25–30 minutes

Material Cards

Preparation Write on separate cards the following words:

hallo	goodbye	boredom	hunger	thirst
madness	OK	money	beauty	love
insult	concentration	secrecy	direction	agreement
anger	pleasure	threat	fear	victory
come here	go away	fatigue	anticipation	approval
disapproval	coldness	heat	good luck	congratulations
begging	disappointment	sincerity	suspicion	bribery
taunting	go slowly	go faster	size	shyness
warmth	difficulty	ease	strength	attention

Note It is better to have more cards than the number of participants. You may like to write more than one card for some words.

1 Form groups of seven or eight. Give about ten to fifteen cards face down in a pile to each group. Ask one person in each group to take one card and without showing it to the others, mime the word marked on it. The others must try and guess what the word is.

2 When someone guesses correctly, encourage the others to discuss the various other ways of expressing this word with a gesture. Note that multilingual groups will have more variations than monolingual ones; allow plenty of time for extensive discussion.

3 When everyone is ready, ask the person who guessed correctly to take the next card and continue as in 1 until all the cards in the pile have been mimed and discussed. You may like to continue this activity by swapping one group's pile of cards with that of another group.

4 Collect all the cards and shuffle. Form groups of three or four and give each group five cards. Ask them to think of a short mime sketch which uses all five words.

5 When everyone is ready, ask each group to perform its mime sketch to the rest of the class. Ask the others to narrate and discuss each sketch in turn.

9 *Language* Present simple; past simple; describing impressions

Vocabulary Non-specific

Level Intermediate   *Time* 25–30 minutes

Material Eight or ten photograph portraits of people; a selection of abstract or artistic photographs

Preparation None

1   Spread the photographs around the room. Ask each student to choose one picture s/he likes and one s/he dislikes.

2   Form groups of six or seven. Ask each student to explain to the others in his/her group why s/he chose these two pictures. Encourage them to talk about their likes and dislikes.

3   Ask each group to choose one portrait. They should discuss who the person is, what he/she does, his/her lifestyle etc.

4   Each group must now invent the life story of the person in the portrait. They should use the pictures which they chose in 1 to illustrate events or moods in the person's life. Encourage them to be as creative as possible.

5   When everyone is ready, ask half the members of each group to visit neighbouring groups to listen to their life stories, while the other half remains behind to narrate its life story to the visitors.

6   Form new groups with one student from each of the old groups. Ask them to try to link all the characters in the portraits into one story or incident, to show that all the characters have played some role in each other's lives.

7   When everyone is ready, each group should narrate its story to the rest of the class. It should be remembered that motivation to listen to the stories will be strong since everyone will be acquainted with the characters; only the story or incident will be different each time.

---

10 *Language* Giving opinions agreeing, disagreeing

Vocabulary Non-specific

Level Intermediate +   *Time* 45–60 minutes

Material None

Preparation None
This is a version of the 'Balloon Game' adapted for language learners

---

1   Explain that three or four famous people are in a hot air balloon. The balloon has a slow leak and one person must be sacrificed to save the others. Each person is going to argue that s/he should be saved by explaining how important or useful s/he is to mankind.

2   Form groups of six to eight. Ask three or four students in each group each to choose a famous person they admire. They should then prepare a list of reasons why this person should be saved or why the other people in the balloon should be sacrificed. The remaining students should act as judges and should prepare a list of questions that they would like to ask the people in the balloon.

23

3 When everyone is ready, the famous people should give their accounts of why they think they should be saved and the others sacrificed. The judges may cross-examine them, and when they have heard all the accounts, they must decide who must be sacrificed for the good of the others.

4 Explain that the balloon is still losing height. Continue as in 3 until there is only one person left in the balloon. Note that the people who have been 'sacrificed' can also act as judges.

5 Explain that the famous people who have survived in each balloon are now to be found in the same balloon. Each one must now justify his/her survival to the whole class who act as judges. They may vote to decide who may live and who must be sacrificed.

---

11. *Language* Past simple; past continuous; making comparisons

Vocabulary Non-specific

Level Intermediate +   *Time* 20–25 minutes

Material Cards; paper (large sheets); dice

Preparation Write on the board the following:

the happiest . . .	the most beautiful . . .
the most frightening . . .	the most tiring . . .
the saddest . . .	the most boring . . .
the most embarrassing . . .	the most interesting . . .
the laziest . . .	the heaviest . . .
the cleverest . . .	the strongest . . .
the funniest . . .	the loudest . . .
the busiest . . .	the kindest . . .

In addition, write up the following sentence:
When I got up this morning, I didn't expect it to be different from a usual working day. However, . . .

---

1 Form groups of two or three. Explain that they are going to make a board game called 'Storytellers'. Give ten cards to each group. Ask them to write on separate cards some of the adjectives shown on the board, and a word or phrase which would go with them, e.g. the happiest day of my life, the most frightening film, the funniest face I have ever seen etc.

2 Collect the cards and shuffle. Form groups of five or six. Give a large sheet of paper and about fifteen cards face down in a pile to each group. Ask the groups to draw two long parallel lines on the paper and to divide this into a hundred numbered squares. They should then mark every fourth or fifth square with an exclamation mark.

3 Ask each student to take an object such as a bus ticket, a button or a matchstick with which to mark his/her progress. Give each group a dice.

4 Each player throws the dice; the person with the highest number starts. He will throw the dice again and move forward the number of spaces indicated. At the same time, he must improvise a story beginning 'When I got up this morning, I didn't expect it to be different from a usual working day. However . . .

5 If, on his first throw, he lands on an exclamation mark, he must pick up the top card (e.g. the most beautiful girl/boy I have ever seen) and introduce the phrase into the story. If he lands on any square other than an exclamation mark, he simply continues describing the weather, what he had for breakfast, how he was feeling etc.

6 While he continues his story, the other players throw the dice and move forward in turn. The person speaking must continue to do so until someone else lands on an exclamation mark. He may not throw the dice while he is speaking. The person who lands on the exclamation mark picks up a card. She continues by integrating the new element into the story.

7 The first player to reach the hundredth square is the winner.

---

12 *Language* Present simple; future simple

Vocabulary Non-specific

Level Intermediate +   *Time* 40–45 minutes

Material Large sheets of paper; cards; dice

Preparation Write on separate cards the following themes:
Romance   Money   Work
Family   Home   Leisure

---

1 Form six groups of roughly equal numbers. Give a theme card and six blank cards to each group. Explain that they are going to make their own fortune-telling board game. Ask each group to write on separate cards three optimistic predictions and three pessimistic ones, all of which should refer to the theme marked on the card.
e.g. You'll meet the most beautiful boy/girl you have ever seen.
Each prediction must include a task.
e.g. Start a conversation and invite him/her for a drink.

2 Collect the cards and shuffle. Give each group a large sheet of paper. Ask them to draw a large square and a smaller one inside. Divide the space between the squares into four equal parts, and then each quarter into thirteen equal boxes. These boxes represent the 52 weeks of the year. Ask them to write in the names of the months.

3 Ask each student to write his/her own initials in ten of the boxes; s/he can place them in boxes which are lying next to each other or completely separate.

4 Each student should take an object such as a bus ticket, a button or a matchstick with which to mark his/her progress through the 'year', and place it at the box representing the first week of January. Give each group approximately equal numbers of prediction cards and a dice.

5 The students play the game by throwing the dice and moving forward the number of spaces indicated. If a student lands on a box containing her own initials, she must pick up a card and perform the task with the player nearest to her on the board, or in the case of two or more players being nearest to her, with the person seated on her left-hand side. The other members of the group judge whether she performs the task well or badly. If she is thought to perform it well, she throws the dice and moves forward the number of spaces indicated, and if she does it badly he throws the dice and moves backwards.

6 When all the prediction cards have been used, swap them with neighbouring groups.

7 The first player to get through the 'year' is the winner.

What's your line?
People and jobs, tools

---

1 *Language* Making requests, agreeing and refusing

Vocabulary Tools, adjectives of size, shape etc.

Level Elementary   *Time* 20–25 minutes

Material Cards

Preparation Write on separate cards the following tasks:

mend a sock	clean the windows	light the fire
wash the dishes	write a letter	make a cup of tea
iron a shirt	make a garden shed	catch a fish
grow some vegetables		

---

1 Form groups of two or three. Give one task card and three blank cards to each group. Ask them to write on separate cards three tools or instruments essential to performing the task.

2 Collect and redistribute the task cards. Collect, shuffle and redistribute the tool cards, three to each group. Explain that each group must think of the tools essential to perform the task it has been given; it may have some or none of the necessary tool cards (if it has all of them, redistribute the cards), so it must try and borrow them.

3 **Variation 1**
The students go round looking for the tools they need to borrow, by describing them but without mentioning them by name.

Variation 2
The students look for the tool they wish to borrow by improvising conversations, into which they introduce the name of the tool as naturally as possible. They may then ask to borrow it. Encourage students to use expressions of agreeing and refusing politely.

4 When a student finds the tool s/he requires, s/he can 'borrow' it by exchanging it for a tool card which s/he does not need. However, if the tool is already being used, it cannot be borrowed.

5 The first group to find all the tools it requires is the winner.

6 You may like to continue this activity by asking the students to prepare their own task cards. Proceed as in 1.

2 *Language* Describing objects; making deductions

Vocabulary Adjectives of size and shape, colour; materials

Level Elementary   *Time* 10–15 minutes

Materials Magazine pictures of machines such as a photocopier, a hot water boiler, a video recorder, a typewriter, a camera, a lawn mower etc.

Preparation Cut each picture into approximately four or five pieces. You may like to stick each piece on to a card. Note that the greater the number of pieces, the more difficult and the longer the game becomes.

1   Give one piece to each student. Explain that these are all pieces of a picture of a machine. Note that unless there are as many participants as pieces, there will be one picture which is incomplete. Ask them to choose words to describe a) the main colour of their piece of the picture, b) the general shape and c) the probable material. Ask them to guess what the machine is likely to be.

2   Ask each student to go round saying the words s/he has chosen to describe the colour. Make sure the piece is concealed. If s/he meets a student who has the same colour, s/he should say the word for the shape and finally for the material. They should then say what they think the machine might be. If they agree, they should continue to look for the rest of the machine together.

3   The group which reconstitutes its jigsaw machine is the winner.

3 *Language* Asking questions; present simple

Vocabulary Jobs

Level Elementary   *Time* 20–25 minutes

Material Cards

Preparation None

This game is a variation on *What's My Line?* adapted for language learners.

1   Form groups of seven or eight. Give each group five blank cards. Ask them to write down on separate cards the title of a job or a profession. Encourage them to be as inventive as possible (e.g. a mounted policeman, a plumber, a tree surgeon etc.). Explain that they are going to mime these jobs to the other members of the group.

2   Ask each group to pass its set of five cards to its neighbour. One person should take a card. S/he has two minutes to mime the job; the others have to guess the title.

28

3 If a group guesses correctly within two minutes, it wins one point.

4 When a group has finished miming all its cards, the game may be continued by swapping its set of cards with another group.

---

4 *Language* Asking questions; present simple

Vocabulary Jobs

Level Elementary +   *Time* 20–25 minutes

Material Cards

Preparation None

---

1 Give a blank card to each student. Ask them to write down the title of the most boring job they can think of (e.g. ballpoint pen tester, onion peeler, art school model etc.). Explain that they are going to mime these jobs to other members of the class.

2 Collect the cards and shuffle. Form groups of seven or eight. Give each group five cards. Continue as in the previous game stage 2.

---

5 *Language* Describing objects

Vocabulary Adjectives of size, shape etc.; materials

Level Intermediate   *Time* 20–25 minutes

Material Cards; magazine pictures of tools (A mail order catalogue is a good source of pictures for this.)

Preparation Cut out pictures of tools and stick them on to cards e.g. an iron, a hammer, a saw. If you do not have time to find pictures, make a list of tools and write each item on a separate card.

---

1 Form groups of approximately equal numbers. Try and keep the groups as far away from each other as possible. Explain that one member of each group will be given a tool, the shape of which s/he has to describe to the others. They must try and draw the shape and guess what tool is being described.

2 Ask one member of each group to come up to you. Take one card and show it to these students. Without speaking, they should return to their groups and describe the shape of the tool as quickly as possible to the others who must draw according to the description. Those who think they know which tool is being described may say its name. If they are wrong, they leave the game for this round.

3 The student who guesses correctly should come to you and tell you what the tool was. If you agree, show him the next card. He returns to his group and continues as in 2.

4 The first group to guess the names of all the tools is the winner.

6 *Language* Asking questions

Vocabulary Jobs, clothing, tools

Level Intermediate   *Time* 15–20 minutes

Material Cards of three different colours

Preparation None

1 Explain that you are looking for clothing and tools which go with specific jobs e.g. butcher – apron – knife. Give one card to everyone and ask them to write down the name of a job.

2 Collect the job cards. Give one card to everyone and ask them to write down the name of a tool or instrument connected with the job they chose in 1.

3 Collect the tool cards. Give one card to everyone and ask them to write down the name of an item of clothing connected with the job they chose in 1. You may need to give the weaker students some help at this point.

4 Collect the cards. Keeping them separate, shuffle each pile. Give one job card, one tool card and one clothing card to each student. Explain that they have to find the tool and the item of clothing which goes with the job. To do this, ask them to decide what might go with the job. Then they should go round asking e.g. 'Do you have a knife?', 'Do you have an apron?' until they find someone who does or until someone offers them something more suitable. Those who find the tool or the item of clothing they require, hand over a card they do not want in exchange.

5 The first person to collect the tool and the item of clothing which go with his/her job is the winner.

7 *Language* Describing use

Vocabulary Non-specific

Level Intermediate   *Time* 15–20 minutes

Material Cards

Preparation Write on separate cards the following:

a jack	an umbrella	a cotton reel
a knife sharpener	a bicycle pump	a pneumatic drill
a grease gun	headphones	a garden roller
a TV aerial	kitchen scales	a telegraph pole
central heating	a photocopier	a headlamp
a bus shelter	a bathplug	a typewriter
a spade	a ruler	a chainsaw

30

On the back of the card, either draw a simple illustration of the object or translate it into the native language of the students.

1 Form groups of roughly equal numbers. Try and keep the groups as far away from each other as possible. Explain that one member of each group will be given the name of a device of some kind. He will then return to his group who will ask him yes/no questions about what it is used for, when it is used, how it works etc.

2 Ask one member of each group to come up to you. Take one card and show it to them. Without speaking, they must return to their groups and reply to the questions with yes/no answers.

3 The student who guesses correctly should come to you and tell you the name of the device. If you agree, show her the next card. She returns to her group and continues as in 2.

4 The first group to guess the names of all the devices is the winner.

---

8 *Language* Making deductions; drawing conclusions

Vocabulary Non-specific

Level Intermediate   *Time* 25–30 minutes

Material Cards

Preparation Write on separate cards the following:
showing people to their seats in the cinema
serving beer in a busy pub
checking tickets in a crowded train
adjusting the TV aerial on the roof of your house
hanging out the washing on a windy day
cleaning the clock face of Big Ben
pouring drinks on a boat in a storm
following a spy along a busy street
interviewing a boring person on a TV programme that is running late
stealing apples from your neighbour's garden

---

1 Form groups of four or five. Explain that one person in each group will mime an activity to the others who must guess what the activity is.

2 Ask one member of each group to come up to you. Take one card and show it to them. Without speaking, they must return to their groups and mime the activity.

3 The student who guesses correctly should come up to you and tell you what the activity was. If you agree, show him/her the next card. S/he returns to his group and continues as in 2.

4 Give one blank card to each group. And them to write a similar activity on the card. It can be one which involves four or five people.

5 Collect the cards, shuffle and redistribute. Explain that each group must prepare a mime sketch based on the activity on the card; it must also try and link its sketch to the sketches of both its neighbours either side. Only one member of each group can negotiate, and only with his/her neighbours; s/he should not hear what the other groups in the sequence are planning to do. The aim is create a coherent mime sequence with as many sketches as groups, but in which no one will know the whole story.

6 When each group is ready, ask the first group to begin. When it has finished its sketch, ask the other groups to describe what they have seen. Encourage as much discussion and speculation as possible until everyone agrees on the meaning of the sketch.

7 Ask the second group to perform the next sketch of the sequence. Continue as in 6 until the whole sequence has been performed.

8 You may like to ask the students to perform the whole sequence again and then ask them to write the story for homework.

---

9 *Language* Giving instructions

Vocabulary Non-specific

Level Intermediate +   *Time* 20–25 minutes

Material Cards

Preparation Write on separate cards the following:

a machine
or device

- to squeeze the toothpaste tube flat
- to water the plants while you are on holiday
- to mow the lawn while you sunbathe
- to sign hundreds of letters with the minimum of effort
- to teach your partner to dance correctly
- to fill up with petrol without stopping at a garage
- to help you eat sandwiches, drink cocktails, smoke a cigarette, shake hands, wipe your mouth and look elegant at parties
- to let you ice skate on a hot summer's day
- to catch flies without hurting them
- to light a cigarette in a strong wind without using your hands

---

1 Form groups of three or four. Give a card to each group. Explain that they must design a machine or a device to perform the function marked on their cards. They may use diagrams and written explanations to show how their invention works.

32

2 Collect the cards and shuffle. Give one card to each group. Ask them to prepare a short sketch which illustrates why they might need the machine or device marked on the card. Make sure that as many members as possible are involved. For example, a group with a 'device to squeeze the toothpaste tube flat' card could prepare a scene early one morning in which one partner in a couple reproaches the other for always squeezing the toothpaste tube in the middle.

3 When everybody is ready, each group should perform its sketch to the whole class. At the end of the sketch, the group which has designed a machine or device to solve the problem portrayed in the sketch should present their invention to the others using the diagrams and the explanation they have prepared in 1.

---

10 *Language* Talking about likes, dislikes and preferences

Vocabulary Jobs, places of work

Level Intermediate +   *Time* 35–40 minutes

Material Postcards of places in which a certain amount of 'human activity' is visible e.g. fishing villages, ski resorts, holiday beaches etc.; cards

Preparation Write on separate cards the following topics:
type of firm/organization
location of job/physical environment
type of work to be done
aspects of work to be avoided
salary and benefits
future prospects

---

1 Form pairs. Give each pair a postcard. Ask them to make a list of all the jobs which the people who live in this place would do. Encourage them to think of all aspects of tourism and commerce. Ask them to count the number of jobs.

2 Each pair should swap postcards with its neighbour. Continue as in 1.

3 The two pairs should tell each other how many jobs they have found. Either pair may challenge the other to justify any job which does not appear on its list.

4 Ask the new group of four to discuss whether any of the jobs mentioned would interest them. Ask them to think about their ideal jobs.

5 Give each group a topic card. Ask them to prepare four or five questions about the topic e.g. type of firm or organization: Would you prefer to work for a private company or for the State? Would you like to work in a large or a small firm? Would you like to be in a company which has contacts abroad?

6 Give each group a letter, A, B, C etc and number the students in each group. Student I from Group A should ask his/her questions to Student 1 from group B, C, D, E etc.

7 When everyone has finished, the whole class should reveal the results of the questionnaire and discuss the topic 'What I like/don't like about work.'

---

11 *Language* Talking about experience

Vocabulary Dates, adjectives for intellectual qualities

Level Intermediate +   *Time* 45–60 minutes

Material Job adverts

Preparation None

---

1 Form groups of three. Ask them to invent the curriculum vitae of someone who is looking for a job. They should write down details of qualifications, work experience, hobbies and interests. It can be based on personal experience or pure invention.

2 Collect the curricula vitae and redistribute them to a quarter of the class. Explain that these students must adopt the identity of the person described in the curriculum vitae. They must study and develop the character as much as possible. Form groups of three with the remaining students. Give each group a job advert. Explain that they are the employers who wrote the advertisement. They must study the advert and develop a clear idea of what the job involves.

3 The employers should display the job advert clearly on the table in front of them. The job-seekers must go round the room looking for jobs for which, according to their curriculum vitae, they might be qualified. They should choose three jobs and leave their names with the employers.

4 The employers should call each candidate for an interview. This should be fairly brief so that there is time to interview everyone who has 'applied' for the job.

5 When the employers have seen all the candidates on their list, they should discuss who would be the most suitable candidate for the job. If the candidate they choose is offered and accepts another job, they must choose someone else.

6 This activity can be continued with a discussion on preparing curriculum vitae, and interview tips and techniques.

12 *Language* Describing necessary skills and qualities

Vocabulary Jobs, personal and professional qualities

Level Intermediate +   *Time* 25–30 minutes

Material Newspaper advertisements for jobs; cards

Preparation Cut the title of the jobs from the job descriptions.

1 Give a job title to one half of the students. Explain that they should think about what the job involves. Give a job description to the other half. Ask them to read it and to guess the title of the job it describes.

2 Ask the students with job title cards to go round describing what the job involves. The others should listen until they find the job title which matches their job description.

3 When everyone has found his/her matching pair, explain that job adverts usually consist of the title of the job, the name or type of company or organization, a description of the tasks involved, the personal and professional qualities required, and the salary and other benefits. Very often the tasks involved are described in a very positive light and the negative aspects aren't mentioned. Ask each pair to discuss the negative aspects of the job in their advert.

4 Give each pair two blank cards. On one of the cards, ask them to write a job title. On the other card, ask them to write a description of this job, which can be either very positive or very negative but should not refer directly to the job. For example:

CHEF
Your job is to entertain and give pleasure to people for two periods of several hours each day, although you will spend longer doing the necessary preparation. You are not usually expected to see any of these people, nor will they usually see you.

5 Collect all the cards and shuffle. Redistribute them. Explain that the people with job description cards should read them and then think of the jobs referred to. They should then go round the room asking yes/no questions to find the person with the matching job card.

6 When they have done this, hand out five blank cards to each pair. Ask them to write on separate cards the name of the place where you would do this job (e.g. factory, bank etc.), and four adjectives to describe professional or personal qualities (e.g. ambitious, clever, efficient, tactful etc.) required for the job.

7 Collect job title cards, place of work cards and adjective cards, keeping the three categories separate. Give a job card to each pair and spread the other cards around the room. Ask them to find one place of work and four adjectives which would refer to their job title card.

Home, sweet home
(Houses, furniture, household items, towns)

1 *Language* Asking questions

Vocabulary Household items

Level Elementary   *Time* 15–20 minutes

Material Pads of paper, pens, cards

Preparation Prepare a list of objects that you would find around the house e.g. a vase, a newspaper, a carving knife, a dish cloth, a teapot stand, a dustbin liner, a curtain rail, a bathplug, a packet of cornflakes, a light switch, a letter box, an ash tray, a tooth brush, a record sleeve, a television aerial. Write each item on a separate card.

1   Form groups of roughly equal numbers. Give each group a pad of paper and a pen. Explain that one person from each group is going to draw an object and the others must try and guess what the object is.

2   Ask one member of each group to come up to you. You take one card and show it to these students. Without speaking, they should return to their groups and draw the object as quickly as possible. The others have to guess what the object is by asking questions. The person who is drawing can only shake or nod his/her head.

3   When someone has guessed what the object is, this person should come to you and tell you what it is called. If you agree that s/he has guessed accurately, you then show him/her the next card in the sequence. S/he returns to his group and continues as in 2.

4   The first group to guess the names of all the objects in the sequence of cards is the winner.

Note The complexity of the objects depends on the level of the group.

2 *Language* Describing objects

Vocabulary Household items, adjectives of size, shape, material etc.

Level Elementary   *Time* 15–20 minutes

Material A number of household objects, such as a box of matches, an elastic band, a tea bag, a key ring, a pair of scissors

Preparation None

1 Form groups of seven or eight. Give each group an object. Divide the group into two sides. Explain that each side must, in turn, think of some phrase or adjective to describe the object. A person from one side must say, for example, 'It's square', and hand the object back to the other side. Someone from this side must take the object and say, e.g. 'It's made of cardboard' and hand the object back. At no point should anyone repeat a description which has already been mentioned.

2 The game continues until one side can no longer add to the description. The other side wins a point.

3 At this point, an object from another group will be passed round, and the game continues with this new object, and so on.

4 The side with the highest number of points is the winner.

---

3 *Language* Describing houses and facilities

Vocabulary Parts of the house, prepositions

Level Elementary   *Time* 10–15minutes

Material None

Preparation None

---

1 Ask the students to draw a plan of one of the rooms of their house or flat, paying particular attention to the shape of the room and the position of the windows, doors and furniture.

2 Form pairs. Ask each student to dictate his plan to his partner without showing it. The partner should try and draw the plan from the oral description without asking any questions or showing her drawing until it is finished. She should then check her drawing with the one made in 1.

3 The partner should then dictate her plan to the first person.

---

4 *Language* Verbs of perception

Vocabulary Adjectives of size, shape, material etc.

Level Elementary +   *Time* 10–15 minutes

Material A number of objects which would be found around the house, e.g. a bottle of perfume, a matchbox, a sponge, a piece of cheese, a cassette, a roll of sticky tape; newspaper; sticky tape

Preparation Wrap each object in a thick layer of newspaper so that its form is difficult to distinguish. Number each object and note down what it is.

1　Form groups of five or six. Give one object to one member of each group. The members of the group should ask Yes/No questions e.g. 'Is it heavy?', 'Is it made of metal?', 'Is it soft?' etc. until they have guessed what the object is. The person answering the questions may not know what the object is, but should nevertheless try to reply as accurately as possible.

2　When the group has either guessed what the object is (or given up), it should ask you what it is. They must not unwrap the object. They should then exchange objects with another group and continue as in 1.

3　At the end of the game reveal the identity of the objects by unwrapping them. The group which has guessed them all correctly is the winner. If more than one group has guessed all the objects, the first to finish is the winner.

---

5 *Language* Describing houses and facilities

Vocabulary Adjectives of size, prepositions, parts of the house

Level Intermediate　　　　　　　　　　*Time* 20–25 minutes

Material Postcards of the buildings mentioned below *or* cards

Preparation If you cannot get the postcards, write on each card the name of a famous building or a monument e.g. the Eiffel Tower, Buckingham Palace, the White House, the Taj Mahal, the Louvre, the Coliseum, the Tower of London, the Empire State Building, the Kremlin, the Parthenon.

1　Form groups of three or four. Number each group and give them a card. Explain that they are estate agents and that their task is to sell the building mentioned on the card. They should prepare a short description of the building, drawing attention to its location, its size, any attractive features, how close it is to the shops, the station etc., and avoiding the unattractive features such as the noise, traffic, the state of repair, age etc. However, the description must *not* mention the name of the building, nor the town where it can be found. Each member of the group should memorize the description.

2　When each group is ready, the students should pass round the room giving their description to the others.

3　When student A has given her description, student B may try and guess the name of the building. If he guesses correctly, he wins two points for his group. If he guesses wrongly, he loses his group two points and passes to the next student. If he cannot guess, he may ask five Yes/No questions. After these, he wins one point for a correct guess and no points for a wrong one. When a student has won or lost points s/he should tell you his/her group's number and his/her score. Keep a note of each group's total scores on the board.

4　The group with the highest number of points is the winner.

6 *Language* Making suggestions; describing houses and facilities

Vocabulary Parts of the house, furniture, prepositions

Level Intermediate   *Time* 20–30 minutes

Material Cards

Preparation None

---

1 Form groups of four or five. Explain that each group is looking for a house or flat which is suitable for all its members to share. Ask them to discuss then write down the five features which seem essential for them all to be satisfied living together in the same home. You may like to suggest the following ideas to encourage the discussion:

type of kitchen	house/flat
type of bathroom/toilets	garden
number of bedrooms	garage
living room/dining room	ground floor/upstairs
neighbourhood	modern/old
shops	town/country
transport	price of rent
recreation facilities	

2 Give each group five cards. Ask them to write each of the five features they have chosen in 1 on separate cards.

3 Each person should take one of these cards and then form new groups of four or five. This new group should prepare a short description of a house or flat which includes all the features mentioned on the cards. They should also invent and add to the description any features they feel would make the house or flat more attractive. This description should be written clearly on a sheet of paper. Note that some features mentioned on the cards will be duplicated; these should be simply emphasized more in the description.

4 The students should return to their original groups. These groups must now begin to look for the house or flat which meets as many of their requirements as possible. When they have read all the descriptions and have chosen the houses or flats which suit them best, they should place their cards beside the description.

5 You should check that the description meets the group's requirements, and award points according to the number of features included in the description.

7 *Language* Describing places

Vocabulary Prepositions

Level Intermediate   *Time* 15–20 minutes

Material A number of street maps of your town. You can usually get these from a local tourist office.

Preparation Cut the maps into seven or eight pieces. Make sure that you cut each map separately so that each piece will be slightly different. Keep each set separate.

Variation 1

1 Form groups of seven or eight. Give one piece of the map to each student. Ask them to look at their pieces and prepare a short description of the parts of the town they include.

2 Ask them to go round giving their descriptions to the other students but without showing the piece until they find its position in relation to the others.

Variation 2

1 Form groups of seven or eight. Take one piece from one set and replace it with a piece from another set. Continue as in Variation 1.

2 Each group must decide which piece does not belong to its set. The person with this piece should try and find the set to which it belongs by questioning the other groups.

8 *Language* Making suggestions; describing facilities

Vocabulary Town facilities

Level Intermediate +   *Time* 30 minutes

Material Cards

Preparation Write on separate cards the following: offices, flats, hotel, sports complex, student residence, luxury houses, park, shopping centre, car park, theatre and library, municipal market building

1 On the board draw a map of the district of town where your school is to be found. Include in the map some of the streets and features of the immediate neighbourhood (e.g. shops, services, monuments etc.). Explain that the district shown on the map is to be redeveloped, which means the school and some other buildings are to be demolished. A number of projects have been suggested and the council is considering them all.

2 Form groups of equal size. One group is to play the role of the council; it must prepare a list of questions which it would like to ask the people who are proposing the various projects in order to learn more about their intentions. Give the other groups a card each, and explain that the project mentioned on it is the one that they are proposing. They must prepare a detailed proposition which outlines the type of development, the need for it in the neighbourhood, the town and the region, the facilities and the potential benefit to the community.

3 When each group has finished its proposition, form new groups with one member from each of the old groups. Each person should in turn present his/her proposition to the representative of the council, who may ask questions.

4 Inform the students that the national government has just passed a law which will only allow new buildings to be built if they are 'of direct benefit to the immediate neighbourhood'. Each group should now discuss exactly how this may affect the propositions and decide which should now be excluded. When each person has finished explaining his/her proposition, the representatives of the council should return to their original group and discuss which proposition seems to be the most suitable for the redevelopment plans.

---

9 *Language* Describing houses and facilities

Vocabulary Parts of the house, adjectives of shape, material etc.

Level Intermediate +   *Time* 25–30 minutes

Material Role cards (see p.15); pictures of houses, flats etc. Note that they can be in varying states of repair

Preparation None

---

1 Form groups of three or four. Give each group a picture of a house. Explain that the group must try and sell it. Ask them to prepare a description of it and, if necessary, invent other details. Point out that even unattractive aspects of the property can be turned into advantages (e.g. 'noisy railway at the end of garden' can become 'close to station'; 'needs decorating' can be 'charmingly old-fashioned' etc.). It should also decide on a price for the property.

2 Give each group a role card. Ask them to discuss the kind of property which would appeal to the person(s) described on the card (e.g. 'young businessman with family' will probably require a house with three bedrooms and perhaps a garden).

3 When everyone is ready, ask two members of each group to visit the other groups and study the property on the market, making notes about features and prices. The remaining members should try

and present an attractive description of their property to prospective buyers.

4   When the buyers have visited all the properties, they return to their group and discuss the details and prices of the property they have seen. Explain that they can only consider houses which are in the same price range of the house they are selling.

5   Those members of the group who stayed behind to sell should now visit the property which interests their group. They should ask detailed questions about the 'advantages' described.

6   They should then return to their groups and decide on a price to offer for the property they particularly like. This can be lower than the price originally asked for.

7   The first group to sell its house and move to something suitable is the winner. If some groups do not manage to do this immediately, they must continue to bargain until they do.

Note For lower or less creative groups, this activity can also be performed using a collection of authentic house advertisements taken from newspapers (e.g. *The Sunday Times, the Observer*) or magazines (e.g. *Country Life, Vogue,*).

---

10 *Language* Making deductions; describing objects

Vocabulary Furniture, parts of the house

Level Intermediate +   *Time* 20–25 minutes

Material Cards; large sheets of card; 8–10 pictures of furnished rooms taken from magazines; several pages of furniture from a mail order catalogue

Preparation Cut out two or three items of furniture from each picture of the furnished room. Stick these on to the cards. Prepare some extra furniture cards cut out from the catalogue pages. Stick the furnished room pictures on to large pieces of card.

---

1   Form groups of three of four. Give half these groups a furnished room picture; these groups are customers. Each group must decide what piece of furniture is missing from its room; note that this is not necessarily obvious from the cut-out shape. Give the other groups a number of furniture cards; these students are shop assistants and the cards represent the stock in their shop.

2   Ask the customer groups to go round the shop groups giving a description of what they think they are looking for; they may guess the probable style as well. The shop assistants must describe what they have in stock. Neither may show the other any of the cards until the shop assistant is sure that s/he has the necessary item of furniture. If the item fits, the customer may keep it. If it does not

fit, the customer must pass directly to the next group without making any further enquiries.

3 The winners are the first group to find all its missing furniture and the shop which has sold the most furniture.

---

11 *Language* Non-specific

Vocabulary Town facilities

Level Intermediate   *Time* 45–60 minutes

Material Cards; blue and red pens; large sheets of paper; dice

Preparation Write on the board the following town facilities:

library	town hall	swimming pool	hospital
dentist	Post Office	park	railway station
school	shopping centre	bank	chemist

and the following 'chance' situations:

BUS   Too crowded – miss a turn.
Road accident – miss a turn.
No money – get off and walk.
New bus lane – move forward 6.
TRAIN Strike – move to nearest bus stop.
Power failure – miss two turns.
Good service – move forward 6.
Train cancelled – move to nearest bus stop.
FOOT You forget your wallet – return home.
You get run over by a car – miss a turn.
You twist your ankle – take a taxi and move forward 12.
A friend gives you a lift – move forward 12.

Note that this game can be based on a real town, using the position of actual facilities and transport routes.

---

1 Form groups of five or six. Explain that they are going to prepare a board game called 'Errands' in which the aim is to run a series of errands as quickly as possible.

2 Give each group a large sheet of paper. Ask them to draw 21 horizontal and 21 vertical lines, making a grid of 400 squares.

3 Ask them to shade in four squares to mark the position of each of the town facilities shown on the blackboard. These may be placed anywhere on the grid.

4 Ask each player to think of three or four errands to run in any of the town facilities and to write them on separate cards, e.g. Go to dentist – have a filling; Go to post office – buy postal order. When everyone has finished, the cards should be collected and placed face down in a pile.

5 Ask them to draw a red line representing the route of the train. This may run through any number of squares on the board. Then

ask them to draw two or three blue lines to represent bus routes. Explain that these may intersect the train route at several points if so desired.

6 Twenty five squares all over the board, including along the train and bus routes, should now be marked with a question mark. These represent 'chance' squares.

7 Ask each group to make a full set of 'chance' situations as shown on the board. They may invent others if they wish to add variety to the game. Each category should be kept separate, placed face down in a pile.

8 Each player should choose a square on the edge of the board which is his/her 'home'. S/He should take an object such as a bus ticket, a button or a matchstick to mark his/her progress. Give each group a dice.

9 The game proceeds as follows: Each player takes an errand card and decides on the quickest way to get to the facility where he carried out the errand.

Each player in turn walks to the nearest bus or train square, moving one square at a time. If he takes the bus, he can move three squares at a time along the bus route; if he takes the train, he can move five squares at a time along the train line; if a player lands on a chance square, she must pick up a chance card and follow the instructions.

A player may change her means of transport only a) when she crosses the route of the bus or train, b) when a chance card allows her to change and c) by throwing an even number on the dice.

When a player reaches the facility, he must choose any member of the group and improvise the dialogue necessary to perform the task. If the other players agree that he has successfully performed his errand, he may take another errand card and continue.

10 The first player to perform six errands successfully is the winner.

Time off
Leisure activities

---

1 *Language* Telling a story

Vocabulary Leisure activities

Level Elementary　　　　　　　　　　　　*Time* 20–25 minutes

Material None

Preparation None

1　Form groups of two or three. Ask them to imagine that they have suddenly become very rich. They should discuss how they would spend a typical Sunday. Ask them to prepare a short mime sketch to illustrate what they would do.

2　When everyone is ready, ask each group to perform its mime sketch to the rest of the class. Encourage the rest of the class to discuss and ask questions about each sequence in the sketch.

3　You may like to ask each group to write up their story for homework.

---

2 *Language* Asking questions; making deductions

Vocabulary Films

Level Elementary　　　　　　　　　　　　*Time* 25–30 minutes

Material Cards

Preparation Write on the board the following film types:

| western | comedy | adventure | romance |
| thriller | horror film | musical | science fiction film |

1　Give a blank card to each student. Ask them to write down the title of a well-known film. Help them to write the English version. Make sure that there are not too many repetitions.

2　Collect the cards and shuffle. Form groups of five or six. Give each group five cards face down in a pile. Explain that one person in each group should take a card and mime the title written on it to the others. They may ask questions but s/he can only reply by nodding or shaking his/her head.

3 The person who guesses correctly takes the next card and continues as in 2.

4 When a group has used all its cards, you can continue this part of the game by giving them its neighbour's used cards.

5 When each group has finished, collect all the cards and shuffle. Draw their attention to the types of film marked on the board. Give a film title card to each student. Ask them to think about the type of film.

6 Explain that all the film titles of one film type must find each other. One student improvises a short dialogue (e.g. at the bus stop, in a restaurant) in the style of her film type (e.g. as a cowboy or a detective). The other student must reply in the style of his film type and the dialogue should continue until they both decide if their films belong to the same type or not. If they do belong to the same type, they should continue their search together until all the films of the same type have been found.

---

3 *Language* Making, accepting and refusing invitations

Vocabulary Sports, sports equipment

Level Elementary   *Time* 5–10 minutes

Material Cards

Preparation Write on separate cards each part of the following compound nouns:

boxing gloves	swimming trunks
tennis racket	golf club
hockey stick	football boots
cricket bat	squash racket
running shoes	

and the following words where the sport is played:

ring	course
pitch	court
pool	court
ground	track
pitch	

---

1 Give one card to each student. Explain that some have names of *sports*, others have words which, when combined with the sport, make up a *piece of equipment*, and others have words for the *place* where the sport is played. Ask students to think of possible sports, pieces of equipment and places which could form a compound noun with the word on their cards.

2 Ask each student to go round the class looking for two partners to play this sport with by improvising a dialogue, introducing into it the word on his card.

47

e.g. 'Hallo! I've got a tennis *court* for 3.30 this afternoon. Would you like to play a game with me?'
The other student accepts or refuses the invitation as appropriate to the sport she is looking for.

3   The first group to find its three partners is the winner.

---

4 *Language* Making deductions

Vocabulary Non-specific

Level Elementary +   *Time* 10–15 minutes

Material Postcards of paintings; try to choose paintings which are not very well-known and which have a title fairly closely related to the content; cards

Preparation Attach temporarily the postcards to larger cards so that the title on the reverse side is obscured. Write each title on separate cards.

---

1   Give half the students a painting each. Ask them to think about what the title might be. Give the other half of the students a title card each. Ask them to think about what the subject of the painting might be.

2   Ask the students with title cards to go round the room asking Yes/No questions to find about the subject of the paintings. They may ask up to twenty questions. A student who is certain that he has found the painting which matches his title may ask the other student to detach her postcard from its backing to look at the title.

3   When everyone has finished, collect the postcards and the title cards and redistribute them so that everyone has an opportunity to look at and discuss all the paintings. Ask the class to discuss which paintings they like and which they dislike. Encourage them to give their reasons.

---

5 *Language* Non-specific

Vocabulary Non-specific

Level Intermediate   *Time* 25–30 minutes

Material Tape recorder; recordings of a number of well-known songs; transcripts of two or three of the songs

Preparation Cut the transcripts into separate lines or verses and stick them on to cards.

---

1   Form groups of four or five. Play a few lines of one of the songs. The first group to give the correct title of the song wins a point.

2   Continue as in 1 with the other songs. The group with highest number of points is the winner.

3 Give a line or verse of the songs to each student. Ask them to go round the room saying or singing the line or verse until they find students with the rest of the song.

4 Ask each group to decide on the sequence of their lines or verses.

5 Play the songs to allow the groups to check on the sequence.

---

6 *Language* Non-specific

Vocabulary Non-specific

Level Intermediate   *Time* 15–20 minutes

Material Tape recorder; the recording of a song; the transcript of the song

Preparation None

---

1 Form three or four groups of equal numbers. Ask the groups to stand in single file; if possible, the board should be at the end of this line.

2 Ask the first members of each group to come forward. Whisper the first line of the song to them; make sure the others in the groups do not overhear. The first members return to their line and whisper to the second person, who turns to the third and so on. The last member of each group writes the line on a piece of paper or on the board. When that person has written the line s/he should come to the front of the line.

3 As soon as one line has passed some way down each group, the first member of each group should come forward (note that this member changes every time a line has been written down) and be given the next line of the song. Continue as in 2.

4 The game continues until the whole song has been written up on the board, each group writing its own version.

5 Ask the groups if they recognize the song.

6 Play the song on the tape recorder and correct one of the versions on the board. The group which makes the least number of mistakes is the winner.

Note that many students enjoy learning the words of songs in English. It is difficult to say which songs are best for this purpose, as this depends on the age and the interests of the group. However, Beatles songs still seem to be the most popular and effective for this purpose.

7 *Language* Giving opinions, agreeing and disagreeing; making suggestions

Vocabulary Numbers, food

Level Intermediate   *Time* 20–25 minutes

Material Copies of a list of calorific values for food

Preparation You may like to make an OHP transparency of the list or just write a selection of the food items and their calories on the board.

1 Form groups of three or four. Ask each group to write down a list of all the things they eat or drink in a day. Give each group a list of calorific values and ask them to add up the number of calories the group consumes in a day.

2 Ask each group to discuss whether they think the diet of its members is healthy or not. Explain that a healthy diet would include about 2000 calories a day, depending on the person's work. Ask each group to discuss how it could cut down on its consumption of food so that each of its members only consumes 2000 calories a day.

3 Ask each group to prepare a day's menu for someone on a diet, including food which would be acceptable to every member of the group. Make sure that they do not exceed 1000 calories.

4 Ask each group to present its menu for the day to the rest of the class. Encourage the others to discuss and criticize the choice of food.

8 *Language* Giving instructions

Vocabulary Food

Level Intermediate   *Time* 20–25 minutes

Material Cards

Preparation None

1 Ask the students to think of their favourite dish. Give each student a blank card and ask them to write down its title.

2 Collect the cards. Give each student a number of blank cards. Ask them to write on separate cards each of the main ingredients of the dishes.

3 Collect the cards and shuffle. Form groups of three or four. Give each group a title card and ask them to discuss which ingredients are essential to make it.

50

4 Spread the ingredient cards around the room and when the groups are ready, ask them to look for the ingredients which they think are essential for their dish.

5 When they have collected the ingredients for one dish, you may like to give them another title card. Continue as in 4.

6 Note that some students may choose the wrong ingredient cards in 4 and 5. Ask each group to place the title card and the ingredient cards on the tables. Each student should check that the dish chosen in 1 has the correct ingredients.

7 You may like to extend this games by asking students to write on separate cards each step of the recipe itself. Collect the cards and shuffle. Spread the recipe cards around the room and continue as in 4.

---

9 *Language* Making, accepting and refusing invitations; giving opinions, agreeing and disagreeing

Vocabulary Adjectives of critical opinion

Level Intermediate   *Time* 25–30 minutes

Material Newspaper advertisements for rock concerts, classical concerts, plays, films, exhibitions, musicals, ballets, operas. Choose an equal number of each type. Cards

Preparation Write on the board the types of entertainment mentioned above.

---

1 Give one advertisement to each student. Ask them to decide what kind of entertainment the advertisements refer to.

2 Explain that they must try and find other students with advertisements for similar types of entertainment. To do this, they must go round inviting people to accompany them to the entertainment.
e.g. *Advertisement for Swan Lake*
A 'I've got two tickets for the ballet next Saturday.'
B 'Oh really?'
A 'Would you like to come? It's said to be very good.'
B 'Oh yes, I'd love to. And I've got two tickets for *Petrouschka* next Monday. Would you like to come . . . ?
or
B – 'No, I'm sorry. I'm afraid I'm washing my hair on Saturday . . .'

3 When everyone has found a partner, give each pair a blank card and ask them to choose one of their adverts. Collect the adverts which are not being used. Ask each pair to write a short comment on the advertised entertainment as if they had just seen it. It should be a critical opinion but should not refer to the entertainment directly.

51

e.g. *Chorus Line* – a musical
'Oh, the singing was wonderful, but I didn't like the dancing very much.'

4 Collect both cards and adverts, and shuffle them. Redistribute them, one to each student. The students with comment cards should think of the type of entertainment which their comment might refer to. Ask them to go round the room saying the comment on their card. The students with adverts should listen and ask questions until they find a comment which matches their advert.

---

10 *Language* Non-specific

Vocabulary Non-specific

Level Intermediate   *Time* 15–20 minutes

Material Cards

Preparation Write the following book titles on separate cards:
Diary of a Madman; *An American Dream*; *The Grapes of Wrath*; *A Farewell to Arms*; *Death in Venice*; *War and Peace*; *The French Lieutenant's Woman*; *Brave New World*; *Around the World in Eighty Days*
Alternatively, you may ask students to choose their own English book titles and to write them on separate cards.

---

1 Form groups of five or six. Ask one member of each group to come up to you. Show them the first card. They should return to their groups and without speaking, mime the title. The others must try and guess the title.

2 The person who guesses correctly should come to you and tell you the title. If you agree, show him/her the next card and continue as in 1.

3 The first group to guess all the titles correctly is the winner.

---

11 *Language* Non-specific

Vocabulary Non-specific

Level Intermediate   *Time* 20–25 minutes

Material Role cards (see p. 15); a number of novels. They should be as varied as possible in content and style. Try and include examples of thrillers, romance, adventure, historical etc.

Preparation None

---

1 Form groups of three or four. Give each group a role card and ask them to think of what the person on their card might enjoy reading. Encourage them to develop the character as much as they like.

2 Spread the novels around the room. Ask the groups to find novel(s) which would appeal to the person on their role cards by reading the publisher's 'blurb' on the back cover.

3 After five or ten minutes, each group should join up again and discuss its recommendations.

4 When everyone is ready, ask each group to present its recommendations to the rest of the class. Ask them first to describe the character of the person on their role cards. They should then explain their choice of novel for this person, giving as much detail about the story and the style as possible. Ask the others to contribute their own ideas on suitable reading matter for this person.

---

12 *Language* Giving opinions, agreeing and disagreeing

Vocabulary Non-specific

Level Intermediate +   *Time* 30–40 minutes

Material Magazine pictures of food, paintings, houses, gardens, people etc.; blank cards; role cards (see p. 15)

Preparation None

---

1 Form groups of three or four. Explain that they are owners of a bookshop which specializes in three or four types of book e.g. Cookery, Art, Novels, Gardening. Ask each bookshop to choose its specialities.

2 Spread the pictures around the room. Ask each group to choose four pictures, each one to represent the illustration on the cover of a book in their bookshop.

3 Each group should now choose a title for their books and prepare a short 'blurb' describing its contents. These should be placed beside the cover illustration.

4 Choose a number of students to become customers and give them a role card each. Explain that they must buy a book which would be suitable for the person described on their role card. Ask them to think about one or two specific types of book which would appeal to this person.

5 When everyone is ready, ask the customers to visit the bookshops to look for a suitable book. The booksellers should answer any questions on the books which interest the customers and even try to convince them that other types of books might be suitable.

6 The first bookshop to sell all or most of its books is the winner.

53

7 If some books are not bought, bookshops may change the titles and the 'blurb' to a type better suited to meet the wishes of certain customers.

13 *Language* Telling a story

Vocabulary Leisure activities

Level Advanced   *Time* 30–35 minutes

Material None

Preparation None

1 Form pairs. Ask each pair to think of a hobby or a sport (e.g. collecting antiques). Explain that they must write a story on any subject which refers to the leisure activity *in an indirect way*.
e.g. 'John got out of his old brass bed and washed his face and hands in the porcelain bowl on the marble-topped washstand. As he went downstairs, the grandfather clock in the hall was striking eight . . .'
The story should be about 100 words long. Encourage them to be as inventive as possible.

2 When everyone is ready, ask each pair to join with a neighbouring pair. One student should begin to read the story. The other pair must try and guess the name of the pastime before the end of the story.

3 As soon as someone guesses the correct name, he and his partner must stop the person narrating each time she says a word which is related to the pastime (e.g. brass bed, porcelain bowl, marble-topped washstand, grandfather clock).

4 When each pair has finished its story, they may pass on to another pair and continue as in 2.

Shopping around
Shops, shopping items, advertising

---

1 *Language* Asking for information

Vocabulary Shops, shopping items

Level Elementary   *Time* 15–20 minutes

Material Cards

Preparation Write on each card one of the following shops:
butcher; baker; chemist; newsagent; greengrocer; tailor; post office; sweet-shop; toyshop; bookshop; shoeshop; hardware store

1 Form groups of four or five. Give a shop card and five blank cards to each group. Ask them to write on separate cards five items which can be bought in this shop.

2 Collect the shop and the item cards. Shuffle the item cards and give one to each student. They may look at the cards but may not show it to anyone else. They must decide where they would buy their items.

3 Ask the students to go round the room asking and answering Yes/No questions, trying to discover what the other students' items are. When one student learns that another student has an item which can be bought in the same shop as his/her own item, they should work together until they have found all five items which can be bought in the same shop.

---

2 *Language* Present continuous for future; making requests, agreeing, refusing

Vocabulary Clothing

Level Elementary +   *Time* 10–15 minutes

Material Cards of two different colours

Preparation Write on separate cards the following items of clothing:

walking boots	apron	ski gloves
dinner jacket	anorak	grey suit
helmet	tennis shoes	ice skates
yachting cap	sunglasses	umbrella
football boots	rubber boots	track suit

55

1 Form pairs. Give a 'clothing' card and a blank card to each pair. Ask them to write on the blank card the occasion on which you might wear the item of clothing

e.g. dinner jacket – a party at Buckingham Palace
sunglasses – a holiday in the sun
rubber boots – a walk in the country

2 Collect all the cards and shuffle. Redistribute them and explain that students (A) with 'occasion' cards must try and find students (B) with the matching 'clothing' cards. Ask students A to think of an item of clothing which they might need for the occasions marked on their cards. They should go round the room improvising a dialogue with students B, i.e. anyone holding a different-coloured card, in which they explain the occasion and ask to borrow the item of clothing required.

e.g. 'Hallo. Sorry to bother you, but I'm having dinner with the Queen next week.'

. . .

'Yes of course I'm looking forward to it. But I haven't got a dinner jacket. Have you got one?'

. . .

'Oh well, never mind' or 'Oh, can I borrow it?'

If student B thinks s/he has another item of clothing which might be suitable for the occasion, s/he may offer it to A who must decide whether this is the correct matching pair by accepting or refusing the offer.

---

3 *Language* Giving instructions; giving opinions; agreeing and disagreeing

Vocabulary Non-specific

Level Elementary +   *Time* 20–25 minutes

Material Advertisements for products or, if possible, the products themselves, which are typically British or typical of your country e.g. Marmite, jelly, salad cream, baked beans, crumpets, seaside rock, lemon curd, clotted cream, mincemeat, biscuits

Preparation None

---

1 Form groups of three or four. Give one product to each group. Ask them to find out what the product is, when it might be used and to discuss whether it would appeal to people in other countries.

2 Ask the groups to imagine that they are in a large department store and that they have to give a demonstration of the product to customers. Each group should prepare a description of the product, giving suggestions and instructions on how and when to use it.

3 When everyone is ready, ask one or two members of each group to visit other groups and listen to the demonstration. Encourage

them to ask questions. The remaining members of the group should give their own demonstration and answer questions.

4   When everyone has seen all the products, discuss with the class which product would be popular if it were marketed in their own country or foreign countries.

---

4 *Language* Giving instructions

Vocabulary Non-specific

Level Intermediate   *Time* 20–25 minutes

Material Cards; the brand names of well-known products such as hair spray, floor polish, instant coffee, disinfectant; sets of instructions taken from the products above

Preparation Stick the instructions on to cards. Blank out all references to the brand name. Write the brand names on cards.

---

1   Form groups of three or four. Spread the brand name cards around the room. Give each group an instruction card. Ask each group to find the brand name which goes with their instructions.

2   Give two cards to each group. Ask them to write down the brand name of another well-known product. On the other card, they should write a short set of instructions on how to use their product.

3   **Variation 1**
Collect the brand name cards and spread them around the room. Collect the instructions cards and give one to each group. They should try and find the brand name which goes with their instructions.

Variation 2
Collect the brand name cards and the instruction cards. Form pairs and give one brand name card to half of the pairs, and instruction cards to the other half. The pairs with instruction cards should guess what kind of product their instructions refer to and prepare a demonstration of how to use this product.
The pairs with brand name cards should go round looking for the matching set of instructions.

---

5 *Language* Giving instructions

Vocabulary Non-specific

Level Intermediate   *Time* 20–25 minutes

Material Cards

Preparation Write on separate cards the following headings for sets of instructions.

How to
- use your cassette recorder
- drive a car
- use the telephone box
- play football
- bathe a dog
- make a cup of tea
- boil an egg
- use a telephone directory

1 Form groups of three or four. Give one card to each group. Ask them to prepare instructions but to replace all the nouns with nonsense words.

2 Ask two members of each group to visit the neighbouring group to give their instructions verbally, taking care to use the nonsense nouns. The group must guess what the instructions are for; they may ask up to five Yes/No questions. If they guess correctly, they must listen to the instructions again and replace the nonsense words with real words. If they do not guess correctly, the people giving the instructions win a point for their group. They then pass on to the next group.

3 When each group has listened to an equal number of instructions, the group with the greatest number of points is the winner.

6 *Language* Present simple; present continuous

Vocabulary Non-specific

Level Intermediate   *Time* 30–35 minutes

Material Cards

Preparation Write on separate cards the names of products and their corresponding advertising slogans. Here are some examples:

Persil	Washes Whiter than White
Gitanes	the French Cigarette
Guinness	Is Good For You
British Airways	Takes Good Care of You
Playboy Magazine	the Magazine for Men
Signal	the Toothpaste with a Smile
Panzani Pasta	Just Like Momma Makes
Brut	After shave for Real Men
Pal	Prolongs Active Life for your Dog

Note that the slogans can either be the real ones or merely representative of the product's advertising style.

1 Give one card to each student. They should go round the room saying the name of the products or the slogan written on the cards until they all find partners.

2 When everyone has found the slogan which goes with the product, form groups of four or five. Each group should choose one of the products and prepare a short mime sketch in the form of a television advertisement which conveys the image of the product.

3 When all the groups are ready, each group in turn should perform its mime to the others who must guess the name of the product.

7 *Language* Making complaints; apologising; making excuses; making suggestions

Vocabulary Shopping items

Level Intermediate   *Time* 20–25 minutes

Material Cards

Preparation None

1 Give one card to each of the students. Ask them each to think of one item that you can buy in shops, maybe the last thing they bought in a shop, for example, and to write it on the card. Then ask them to think of what could go wrong with this item and to write the defect on the card.
e.g. WRISTWATCH – loses time, WASHING MACHINE – leaks water

2 Collect the cards and shuffle them. Give one card to half the students. Explain that they have just bought the items marked on the cards and that there is something wrong with them. Tell the other students that they are the assistants in the shop where the items were bought. The shoppers must go to any assistant and complain that the item they have just bought is defective. The shop assistant must be very polite, make excuses but deny responsibility and claim that it is really the fault of the neighbouring shop assistant. The shopper must then go to the nearest shop assistant, explain what is wrong with the item and inform him or her of what the first shop assistant said.

3 The game continues until the shop assistant can no longer think of any excuses to make and concedes defeat.

8 *Language* Making suggestions; talking about likes and dislikes

Vocabulary Money

Level Intermediate   *Time* 20–25 minutes

Material Role cards (see p. 15); blank cards; pages from newspapers or magazines advertising Christmas presents. Make sure that the prices are included.

Preparation None

1 Give a role card and a blank card to each student. Ask them to think about the character and develop an idea of his/her likes and dislikes. They should write down a brief description on the blank card of this person's interests as if they were a close friend or relative.

e.g. *Aunt Mary*: likes theatre, flower arranging, collecting antiques, history books. Dislikes modern design, fashion and pop music.

2 Collect the role cards and put them aside. Collect the cards describing the person's likes and dislikes and shuffle. Form groups of three or four. Give three or four cards and a page or two of Christmas presents to each group. Ask them to look for presents which would be suitable for the people on their cards. Explain that they only have £20 to buy all the presents.

3 When everyone is ready, ask each group to present a description of the people on their cards and to explain what presents they have chosen. Encourage the others to comment on the choice and make other suggestions for suitable presents using their own adverts.

---

9 *Language* Describing use

Vocabulary Non-specific

Level Intermediate +   *Time* 15–20 minutes

Material Cards

Preparation Write on separate cards the following:
A slice of stale bread
An old dish cloth
A car without any wheels
A used ballpoint pen
A half-eaten apple
An out-of-date season ticket
A bunch of dead flowers
A broken umbrella
A bent nail
An empty whisky bottle
Alternatively, you may like bring to class any useless objects you may find at home.

---

1 Form groups of two or three. Give each group an object or an object card. Explain that they are salespeople who have to sell this object. They must think of convincing reasons to buy this object and why it would be useful to customers. Encourage them to be as inventive and humorous as they like.

e.g. **A bent nail**
'Have you ever found yourself doing those jobs around the house which seem to need more fingers and thumbs than you actually

have? Or have you had to paint the ceiling while standing on tiptoe at the top of a shaky ladder? Or clean the outside of top floor windows from the inside? You never seem to be able to find the right tools for the right job, do you? One of the most difficult household tasks is to nail carpets or pieces of wood when you don't have enough room to use the hammer properly. So when the job is less than straightforward, use our famous BENT NAILS, for hammering round corners . . .'

2 Ask each group to prepare a short TV commercial for their product. They should try and use all the members of the group either as presenters of the product's different uses or as narrators of the advert itself.

3 When everyone is ready, each group should present its TV commercial to the rest of the class.

---

10 *Language* Describing objects; making suggestions; making comparisons

Vocabulary Non-specific

Level Intermediate +   *Time* 20–25 minutes

Material Cards; newspaper or magazine advertisements for a number of different products, e.g. cars, typewriters, cookers, tape recorders, washing machine, bedroom or bathroom suites etc.
   Each product should have a set of three different adverts e.g. car – adverts for a Renault 5, a Ford Fiesta and a Volkswagen Golf.

Preparation Write on separate cards a brief description of the product from the point of view of a prospective customer:
e.g. car – fairly cheap, low petrol consumption, small but reliable, easy to get spare parts, large boot etc.
Note that there will be one product card for each set of advertisements.

---

1 Give out the product cards to individual students. Explain that they are potential buyers of the product marked on their card. Ask them to prepare some ideas on why they are hoping to buy the product, when and where they intend to use it, how much they can afford to spend etc. Form groups of two or three with the remaining students. Give each group a set of advertisements. Explain that they are advisers on consumer affairs. Ask them to prepare a comparative study of the three advertisements. They should compare prices, size, durability, special features and think about the kind of customer to which each advertisement would appeal.

2 When everyone is ready, direct the customers to the relevant group of advisers. Ask the customer to explain to the advisers exactly what s/he is looking for. The advisers should ask questions and give their advice on what to buy.

11 *Language* Non-specific

Vacabulary Shopping items

Level Intermediate +   *Time* 10–15 minutes

Material Cards of two different colours

Preparation On separate cards write the names of any well-known product which is being advertised at the moment, e.g. Ajax, Marlboro, Signal

1   Form pairs. Give each pair a product card and a different coloured blank card. Ask them to write on the blank card a word or short phrase which has a connotation with the product, e.g. Ajax – White Strength, Marlboro – Cowboy, Signal – Stripes.

2   Collect the cards and shuffle. Give one card to each student. Explain that the students with connotation cards should try and find the students with the matching product cards. To do this, the student must first think of the name of the possible product, and without showing her card, should go round the room improvising conversations with any student with a different coloured card. She must try and introduce the connotation word or phrase as naturally but as quickly as possible.
e.g.   A 'Did you see the film last night?'
         B 'No, I didn't.
         A 'Oh, you missed a very good film. It was a Western, you
              know, with *cowboys* and Indians . . .'
The student with the product card must also try to think of the possible connotation word or phrase. If he hears it in the dialogue, he may show his card and challenge the other to do likewise. If the challenge is unsuccessful, the players continue until they find their matching pairs.

12 *Language* Non-specific

Vocabulary Non-specific

Level Intermediate +   *Time* 10–15 minutes

Material Magazine pictures without captions (Avoid using advertisements); cards

Preparation None

1   Form groups of two or three. Give one picture to each group. Ask the students to think of the product which this picture might be advertising. They must think of the possible advertising slogan and write it on a blank card. They must not mention the name of the product.

2 Ask each group to prepare an oral description of their product, e.g. who would use it, where you would see it, when you would use it, how often etc. but without being too specific and without mentioning the name of the product. However, they must be truthful at all times. Suggest that they give a detailed description of the product being used in a typical situation. They should divide the description into three paragraphs.

3 Each group should join up with a neighbouring group. Displaying the slogan but not the picture, group A should give the first part of its description to group B, who have to guess what the product might be. Group B may ask three questions after the first part of the description. If it guesses the name of the product, it wins three points. If it doesn't, Group A continues with the second and third parts of the description; Group B may ask further questions after each part, winning two points or one point if it guesses correctly.

4 Group A should then pass on to Group C etc. Continue as in 3.

5 The group with the highest number of points is the winner.

---

13 *Language* Asking for information

Vocabulary Shopping items

Level Intermediate +   *Time* 10–15 minutes

Material Cards

Preparation Write each of the following British English words on separate cards in blue ink, and their American English equivalents in red ink.

UK	US	UK	US
anorak	parka	hair slide	barette
aubergine	egg plant	handbag	pocket book
biscuits	cookies	mackintosh	raincoat
braces	suspenders	minced meat	ground beef
jumper	sweater	nappy	diaper
chips	French fries	pushchair	stroller
sweets	candy	spanner	monkey wrench
courgettes	zucchini	suspenders	garters
crisps	chips	tights	pantie hose
curtains	drapes	torch	flashlight
drawing pins	thumb tacks	vest	undershirt
dressing gown	bathrobe	waistcoat	vest
dungarees	overalls	pants	shorts
plimsolls	sneakers	trousers	pants

1 Shuffle the cards carefully and give one to each student. Explain that the students with a card written in blue are British tourists in the United States of America, and that they are looking for the item written on the card in the shops. They must go round the room

asking e.g. 'Do you have an anorak?' until they find the person with the matching American English card.

2 It is a good idea to place all the cards on the table so that everyone can take a good look at all the different words.
Note This activity can be performed with other vocabulary items e.g. transport.

On the road
Tourism and travel, tourist facilities

---

1 *Language* Describing places

Vocabulary Geographical description

Level Elementary   *Time* 15 minutes

Material Postcards or pictures of the countryside or coast

Preparation None

---

1 Form groups of nine to twelve. Each group should then be divided into three sub-groups, each with three or four students. Give one picture to each sub-group. Ask them to note down as many items of vocabulary as they can find in the picture.

2 When each sub-group has finished, it should exchange pictures with its neighbour. Continue as in 1 until each sub-group has noted down the vocabulary from all the pictures in the group.

3 The sub-group with the greatest number of correct words is the winner.

---

2 *Language* Describing places

Vocabulary Parts of the town; countries

Level Elementary   *Time* 5–10 minutes

Material Postcards or pictures of well-know cities or sights, buildings or monuments (e.g. the Eiffel Tower, the Empire State Building, the Sugar Loaf Mountain etc.)

Preparation None

Variation 1

1 Form pairs. Give a picture to one student in each pair. Without showing it to the other, s/he must give a description of the town or country where you would find the scene shown in the picture. The other student must try and guess where it is.

2 When they have finished, give a different picture to the other student. Continue as in 1.

65

Variation 2

1 Form pairs. Give a picture to one student in each pair. The other student must ask Yes/No questions to discover the town or country shown in the picture.

2 When they have finished, give a different picture to the other student. Continue as in 1.

---

3 *Language* Past simple

Vocabulary Nationalities, countries

Level Elementary +   *Time* 20–25 minutes

Material Cards

Preparation None

---

1 Give each student a card. Ask them to think of a country and a typical thing to do in this country. They should write a sentence on the card saying where they went on holiday and what they did there.
e.g. I went to Holland and bought some tulips.
     I went to Paris, and went up the Eiffel Tower.
     I went to China and learnt to eat with chopsticks.
They should also write down the adjective to refer to the country, the noun for the person from the country, and the noun to refer to the nation as a whole. Explain that these are not always the same words e.g. *Dutch*, a Dutchman, the Dutch. Offer to help individual students who do not know the correct words, and check that the others have written them correctly.

2 Collect the cards and shuffle. Form groups of six. Give each group six cards. Explain that one person in each group is going to take one card and mime what is written on it. The others in the group have to guess where s/he has been on holiday and what s/he has done. The group score one point if they guess correctly, and one point for each correct 'nationality' word.

3 The person who guesses correctly takes the next card and continues as in 2, and so on until all the cards have been used.

4 The group with the highest score at the end of the game is the winner.

5 It is a good idea to make a list of all the words on the board at the end of the game.

4 *Language* Present tenses; describing places

Vocabulary Geographical description

Level Elementary +   *Time* 20–25 minutes

Material A number of holiday postcards; pictures from travel agents brochures, magazines etc.

Preparation None

1   Explain to the students that you have just received a postcard from a friend who is having a holiday in an exotic foreign country. As you read the following text aloud, illustrate it with five or six pictures. (Note that it can be amusing to use pictures which contradict the text):
'The weather here in San Serif is wonderful (picture of pouring rain) and the beaches are fabulous (picture of crowded beach). The food is very good and very different from what you can get back home (picture of a hamburger). There's lots to do in the evening (pictures of empty streets at night) and I've made some very nice friends (picture of punks). See you next week . . .'

2   Spread the pictures around the room. Form groups of three or four. Give each group a postcard. Ask them to discuss the scene shown.

3   Ask each group to choose five or six pictures. They should then invent a text for their postcard.

4   When everyone has finished, ask each group to read out its 'illustrated postcard' to the rest of the class.

---

5 *Language* Making suggestions, agreeing and disagreeing

Vocabulary Tourist facilities, prepositions

Level Elementary +   *Time* 20–25 minutes

Material None

Preparation Write on the board the following tourist facilities:
Ski resort – 1 square, swimming pool – 1 square, hotel – 2 squares, flats – 2 squares, car park – 2 squares, artificial lake – 4 squares, Golf course – 4 squares, cinema/theatre/disco – 2 squares, tennis court / 1 square

---

1   Form an equal number of groups of two or three. Ask each group to prepare two copies of an imaginary country region. They should draw suitable symbols representing the various geographical features such as rivers, mountains, forests, villages, railways, roads.

2   When everyone is ready, explain that they are going to develop the region for tourism and that a major leisure complex is going to be

67

built. Ask the group to divide both copies of the map into 144 squares by drawing 11 vertical lines and 11 horizontal lines. They should write a letter above each square along the horizontal line at the top and a number by each square down the vertical line on the left hand side.

3 Ask each group to consider the most suitable places to position the tourist facilities which are marked on the board. For example, the main complex of hotels and shops should be placed near an existing access road and the car park should be close by. When they have decided where to place them, they should shade in their position on *one* copy of the map, using only the number of squares marked on the board.

4 When everyone is ready, ask each group to turn to its neighbour. Each group should give the other the copy of the map *without* the facilities marked. Explain that each group has to find out where the other has positioned its facilities by calling out a letter and a number.

5 Group A should study the map and decide where group B might have positioned its various facilities. It will call out a letter and a number e.g. A7. Group B will say whether this square has been filled in or not. Group B then calls out a letter and a number and group A will reply. After twenty-five calls each, each group should try and deduce from the squares filled where the facilities have been positioned.

---

6 *Language* Describing places and facilities, asking for information

Vocabulary Geographical description, parts of the town

Level Intermediate   *Time* 20–25 minutes

Material Travel brochures; role cards (see p. 15)

Preparation None

---

1 Form groups of three or four. Give half the groups a travel brochure. Explain that they are travel agents and should study the brochure in order to give information about the various holidays to prospective customers. Ask them to think about the holidays and what kind of people they might appeal to. Give the other groups a role card. Explain that one person on their role card is looking for a suitable place to go on holiday. Ask them to think about the kind of holiday which would appeal to this person.

2 When everyone is ready, ask the prospective customers to go round the travel agents asking for information about the various holidays they are offering. They should ask detailed questions about the holidays which the travel agents must try and answer.

3 When the customers have visited all the travel agents, they should join up and discuss the various possibilities. Ask the customers to tell the whole class which holiday they have chosen and explain their reasons why.

4 The travel agent to sell the greatest number of holidays in the winner.

---

7 *Language* Making suggestions; agreeing and disagreeing

Vocabulary Parts of the town

Level Intermediate   *Time* 40–45 minutes

Material Cards; dice; large sheets of paper

Preparation None

---

1 Form groups of four or five. Explain that they are going to prepare a game called 'Time Off'. Give each group ten cards and ask them to think of a town they know well. Ask them to choose five places or sights in the town which a tourist might like to visit, and five places or sights which a tourist would be well-advised to avoid. Note that these places need not be famous tourist spots; they can be favourite restaurants or a place where there are heavy traffic jams. Each place should be written on separate cards.

2 Give each group a large sheet of paper. Ask them to draw two parallel lines in the shape of an S and to divide this into a hundred squares. They should then mark an exclamation mark in ten separate squares all over the board. Ask them to shuffle the cards and place them in the centre of the board.

3 Ask each player to take an object such as a bus ticket, a button or a matchstick to mark his/her progress. They should place these objects at the start.

4 The game proceeds as follows: Each player throws the dice in turn, moving the number of squares indicated. Anyone who lands on an exclamation mark must pick up a card. A place to see gives a move forward of three squares; a place to avoid means a turn must be missed.

5 The first player to finish the course is the winner.

---

8 *Language* Asking for information; describing facilities;

Vocabulary Tourist facilities

Level Intermediate   *Time* 20–25 minutes

Material Brochures and guides of a number of different towns; role cards (see p. 15)

Preparation None

---

1 Form groups of three or four. Give half the groups a brochure of a town. Explain that they are the staff of a Tourist Information office in that town. They should read the brochure and learn as much as possible about the town. Give the other groups a role card. Explain that the person on their card is visiting a town for the first time. Ask them to think of places to see and things to do which would appeal to this person.

2 The groups with role cards should visit the Tourist Information offices asking for advice on what there is to see and do in that particular town. Each group should visit all the offices.

3 When the whole group has visited all the offices, it should join together again and discuss which town would most appeal to the person on their role card.

4 Ask each tourist group to tell the rest of the class which town it has chosen. Find out which town is the most popular with the tourists.

---

9 *Language* Describing places; giving directions

Vocabulary Geographical description

Level Intermediate   *Time* 20–25 minutes

Material A number of maps of different regions. Ordnance Survey-style maps are ideal for this purpose.

Preparation None

---

1 Form groups of six or seven. Give each group a map and a number of cards. Ask each group to look at the map and to choose a tour which passes through six or seven clearly-marked reference points (towns, landmarks etc.). Ask them to write down two consecutive reference points on separate cards (e.g. St Mary's village – Blackmoor Down, Blackmoor Down – Layham's farm, Layham's farm – Alton forest etc.). If they wish, the tour can finish at the point where it began. They should number the sequence of the cards.

2 Each group should exchange maps and cards with its neighbour. Each student should take a card and without showing it to the others in the group, find out where the two references points are positioned on the map.

3 The student with the first card should give a detailed description of the route to take between his two reference points without mentioning the name of his destination. When he has completed his description, the rest of the group will have arrived at the starting point of the next student's description. She should continue the tour. This continues until the tour has been completed.

70

10 *Language* Making suggestions; asking for help

Vocabulary Non-specific

Level Intermediate   *Time* 20–25 minutes

Material Cards

Preparation Write on separate cards the following situations:
You have been overcharged in a restaurant.
You can't find your way back to your hotel.
You've been bitten by a mad dog.
You've lost your passport.
You've missed your flight home.
You have to send a telegram to tell someone you've missed your flight.
Your gold watch was accidentally thrown away with the rubbish.
You've worn your shoes out by too much sightseeing.
You accidentally posted an envelope containing all your holiday money.
You can't turn the tap off in your hotel room.
You left your suitcase on the train.
Your husband/wife has been locked in the Underground late at night.
Your husband/wife is in a rubber boat at sea, and it's sinking.
An elephant at the zoo has taken the bag with your lunch in it.
The steering wheel of your car has just come off in your hands.
Write on separate cards the following job titles:
   restaurant manager; policeman; doctor; consulate official; airline represen-
   tative; post office official; dustman; shoe shop assistant; postman; cham-
   bermaid; lost property official; Underground station manager; lifeguard; zoo
   keeper; garage mechanic

1 Ask the class about the worst experiences which have ever
   happened to them while they have been in a country where they
   could not speak the language.

2 Give half the class situation cards and ask them to imagine that
   they are in that situation in a foreign country. Ask them to think
   about what they would do and who they would ask for help. Give
   the other half of the class job titles and ask them to think of what
   kind of things they might have to do in the job.

3 Ask the tourists to go round miming the situation to anyone with
   a job card. The student with the job card must try and guess what
   situation the tourist finds himself in. When she has done so, she
   should mime her job. They must both decide whether the student
   with the job title card can help the tourist. If they decide she cannot,
   the tourist should continue to look for someone who can.

4 The first tourist to find someone to help him is the winner.

71

11 *Language* Non-specific

Vocabulary Countries

Level Intermediate +   *Time* 40–45 minutes

Material Atlas; dice; cards; large sheets of paper

Preparation None

1   Form groups of five or six. Explain that they are going to make a board game called 'Destinations'. Give each group a large sheet of paper and ask them to draw a map of the world; the map does not have to be accurate, merely recognizable.

2   Ask them to draw horizontal and vertical lines which divide the map into approximately 1-inch squares.

3   Give ten cards to each student. On five of these cards ask them to write the names of five towns around the world which they would like to visit. Encourage them to choose a variety of different destinations. They should mark the position of these towns clearly on the map; they can consult the atlas if necessary. On the other five cards, they should write five typical activities to do in these towns, such as places to visit or sights to see. Encourage them to choose the most typical activity they can think of for each town.

4   Collect the town cards and shuffle them. Give five to each player. These cards represent the places along the route which s/he is going to take around the world. Although it is not essential for the game, it is more interesting if each player gets different towns. Note that all the players will have different routes to take. Ask them to decide on the quickest route to each all these towns. Collect the activity cards and shuffle. Give five to each player.

5   Ask each student to take an object such as a bus ticket, a button or a matchstick to mark his or her progress, and to choose a town anywhere in the world which is 'home'. Place the object in this square.

6   The object of the game is for each player to go right round the world as quickly as possible, visiting the six towns on his or her cards, and 'performing' an appropriate activity in each one.

7   The game proceeds as follows:
The players throw the dice in turn moving the number of squares indicated in any direction (They may not move diagonally). They should aim for the first town on their route.
If a player throws a six, she may 'take a plane' directly to her destination. If a player has to cross the sea at any point, he must 'wait for the boat' until he has thrown a two or a four. (Of course,

if he throws a six, he can take a plane). If he is unsuccessful in throwing an even number, he must wait for his next turn.

When a player reaches any of the towns along her route round the world, she must think of a typical activity to do there. She then improvises a conversation with any one of the other players by saying what she intends to do there. If the other player has a card with this activity marked on it, he must hand it over and receive another activity card in exchange. The player may now proceed to the next town on her route. If the other player does not have the card, the first player must wait until her next turn and either try the conversation with another player, or think of another typical activity to do in this town. It may be, of course, that the player has already got the card appropriate to her present position; in this case, she should show it to the others. If everyone agrees, she may proceed directly to her next destination.

8   The players should continue all the way round the world, visiting all the towns on their routes, until they arrive back home. The first player to do so is the winner.

7 Read all about it!
The press, current affairs

1 *Language* Making suggestions; agreeing and disagreeing; making deductions

Vocabulary Non-specific

Level Elementary   *Time* 10–15 minutes

Material Pictures of topical interest taken from newspapers and magazines

Preparation None

1 Form groups of four of five. Give one student in each group a picture without showing it to the others. They must ask Yes/No questions to discover the subject of the picture.

2 When the group has discovered the subject of the picture ask them to discuss the item of news which it illustrates. They should also think of the headline or caption to the picture.

3 Ask them to think of the circumstances which led to what is shown in the picture. They should prepare an interview with some or all of characters connected with the news item. Some of the students should play the role of the journalists, the others should play the role of the people involved in the story.

2 *Language* Giving opinions; agreeing and disagreeing

Vocabulary Non-specific

Level Elementary   *Time* 15–20 minutes

Material Pictures, headlines and articles concerning matters of topical interest.

Preparation Separate the pictures, headlines and articles from each other.

1 Give a headline to half of the students and a photograph to the others. Ask the students with the headline to go round saying it aloud to the others who must decide whether it refers to their pictures or not. When two students find they have a matching pair, they should show headlines and pictures to each other.

2 Ask each pair to discuss the item of news to which their picture and headline refers. Ask them to decide whether the news item is

up-to-date or a few days (or more) old. They should note down as many details of the news item as they can remember.

3 Spread the articles around the room. When each pair is ready, ask them to look for the article which matches their headline and picture. When they have found it they should read it through carefully and check that the notes they made in 2 are correct.

3 *Language* Asking questions; telling a story

Vocabulary Non-specific

Level Intermediate   *Time* 40–45 minutes

Material Headlines and the corresponding articles

Preparation Cut the headline from the article. Stick them on separate cards.

1 Form groups of two or three. Give one card to each group. Explain that the groups with headlines are reporters. Ask them to discuss the subject of their story from what they can infer from the headline. They should prepare a list of questions which they would like to ask the people involved in the story. Explain that the groups with the articles are the people involved in the story. Ask them to read the article and to make sure they learn the details. If they wish, they may all adopt the role of the same character in the story. They should be ready to answer detailed questions.

2 When everybody is ready, the reporters must try and find the people involved in their story by going round the room saying who they think they are looking for. The others should only identify themselves when they meet a reporter who has guessed correctly.

3 When the reporters have found the people they are looking for, they should interview them individually. The reporters should each take notes on any aspect of the incident which would be interesting enough to be included in an article.

4 Ask the reporters to compare notes and to check whether the people they have just interviewed have all told exactly the same story. If there are any variations, the reporters may ask further questions.

5 The reporters should now write a short report of the story with the help of the people involved.

4 *Language* Non-specific

Vocabulary Non-specific

Level Intermediate   *Time* 15–20 minutes

7

Material Articles taken from all sections of the newspaper (e.g. home news, foreign news, arts, business, sport, TV and radio etc.); the contents column of a newspaper

Preparation Write the contents column of the newspaper on the board.

1 Spread a large number of different articles around the room. Ask students to read as many articles as possible for gist understanding.

2 Draw their attention to the headings on the board. Explain that these are the headings of the main sections of a newspaper. Ask them to group all the articles together under the relevant heading.

3 Ask the class if they think that a newspaper should have more or fewer sections. Which sections are of most interest to them, and which ones do they never read?

---

5 *Language* Making suggestions; agreeing and disagreeing

Vocabulary Non-specific

Level Intermediate   *Time* 20–25 minutes

Material Newspaper articles of topical interest without the headlines; cards

Preparation None

---

1 Form groups of two or three. Give each group an article. Ask them to read it and to decide which are the most important points in it. They should take notes.

2 Ask them to use their notes to write a short newspaper headline for the article. Explain that it should avoid using 'structural' words such as auxiliaries and articles unless they are absolutely necessary for the sense.

3 Give each group a number of cards. Ask them to write down on separate cards each word of their headline.

4 Collect the cards and shuffle. Spread them around the room. Collect the articles and redistribute them, one to each group. Ask the groups to read the article and to think of the headline which should accompany it.

5 When everyone is ready, ask the groups to look for the words they need to reconstitute the headline for their article. If at any point someone from another group wants a word card which they have already chosen, members of each group should try and justify their choice to the other.

6 *Language* Telling a story

Vocabulary Non-specific

Level Intermediate *Time* 25–30 minutes

Material Gossip columns from a variety of newspapers; cards

Preparation Write on the board the following:
1 Where they were
2 What she was wearing
3 What he was wearing
4 What they were doing
5 What happened then

1 Form groups of five. Explain that a gossip column is a section of a newspaper which reports on the social life of famous people. Ask the students if this kind of journalism occurs in any form in their own country. Which newspapers specialize in gossip columns?

2 Give each group an example of a gossip column. Ask them if they know any of the people mentioned in it. If so, what else do they know about these people?

3 Give each student two cards. Ask them to write on separate cards the names of two famous people, one male and one female. Explain that these two people do not need to be connected in any way.

4 Collect the male cards and shuffle. Give one to each group. Collect the female cards and shuffle. Give one to each group. Explain that each group is going to write a short article about these two people for a gossip column. Ask each group to take a sheet of paper. The first student should look at the board and then write down what *she* was wearing. Encourage the students to be as inventive as possible. When he has finished he should fold the paper so as to conceal what he has written. The second student should look at the board and then write down what *he* was wearing. She should then fold the paper. This should continue until all the members of the group have written a sentence about these two people.

5 When the group has finished, it should unfold the piece of paper and read out the article.

6 Ask them to rewrite the article in a similar style to the real gossip column they read in 2.

7 Ask each group to read out its article to the rest of the class. You may like to pin all the articles to the wall.

7 *Language* Making deductions

Vocabulary Politics

Level Intermediate   *Time* 15–20 minutes

Material Political cartoons from newspapers with captions

Preparation Cut the cartoons from their captions.

1 Form groups of three or four. Give each group a cartoon. Ask them to discuss what the cartoon refers to, who the characters are, what is happening etc.

2 Ask the groups to think what the caption to the cartoon might be.

3 Spread the captions around the room. Ask the groups to look for the caption which matches their cartoon. When they have found it, ask them to place the cartoon next to the caption.

4 Encourage the groups to look at all the cartoons and captions. Ask them which ones they find most effective.

8 *Language* Making deductions; expressing probability

Vocabulary Non-specific

Level Intermediate   *Time* 10–15 minutes

Material Strip cartoons such as Schultz or Bretecher. Choose cartoons which have six or more separate drawings.

Preparation If you are using cartoons in a language other than English, blank out the words. Cut each cartoon into separate drawings. Stick them on cards.

Variation 1

1 Shuffle the drawings and give one to each student. Ask the students to prepare a brief oral description of the drawing.

2 Ask the students to go round the room giving descriptions of the pictures, looking for students who might be describing drawings from the same cartoon sequence.

3 When a number of students think they have drawings from the same cartoon, they should try and decide on the correct sequence. They can only show the drawings when they are sure that they have done this successfully.

Variation 2

1 Take one drawing from each cartoon strip and replace it with one from another. Form groups of three or four students. Give one set of pictures to each group. Ask them to reconstruct the sequence and decide which drawing is the odd-man-out.

2 Each member of the group should go round the other groups giving a description of the odd-man-out, until the strip cartoon which it belongs to is found.

3 When all the strip cartoons have been reconstructed, they should be laid out on the table for everyone to see.

---

9 *Language* Telling a story; making deductions

Vocabulary TV programmes, adjectives of critical opinion

Level Intermediate   *Time* 40–45 minutes

Material The television guide from several newspapers

Preparation Cut out the titles of a number of television programmes and stick them on cards. Stick the commentaries of these programmes on cards.

---

1 Give one card to each student. Explain that the students with title cards must try and find the students with the matching commentaries. Ask them to decide on the type of programme. They should then go round the room asking Yes/No questions to anyone with a commentary card until they find their partner.

2 Ask each pair to use the commentary to help them to work out a short sketch from the programme.

3 Ask each pair to give a brief description of their programme to the rest of the class. The whole class should then discuss the possible order of these programmes as if they were all to be shown during one evening of television viewing.

4 Ask one person to act as the presenter of the programmes. S/he should introduce each one in turn.

5 Ask each pair to present its sketch to the others.

---

10 *Language* Giving opinions; agreeing and disagreeing

Vocabulary Non-specific

Level Intermediate   *Time* 35–40 minutes

Material Cards; examples of various newspaper competitions, particularly the kind in which you are asked to put various statements in order of priority.

Preparation Write on separate cards the following:
Win a new car
Win a house in the South of France
Win a holiday in the Bahamas
Win a candlelit dinner for two
Win a luxury yacht
Win a cruise in the Pacific
Win a caravan
Win a weekend for two in the town of your choice

1 Form groups of five or six. Give each group a newspaper competition. Ask them to place the features or statements in what they consider to be the correct order of importance. There is often a sentence to complete at the end of the competition. They should do this.

2 Give each group a competition card. Using the competition in 1 as a model, ask them to prepare their own competition. They should make their own list of features and make note of what they consider to be the correct order of importance. They should also prepare a sentence to complete.

3 Ask the groups to pass their competitions around the other groups. They should prepare their answers on a separate sheet of paper and include the names of their members.

4 When they are ready, ask each group to decide whether the features of the competition which they have prepared have been placed in the right order. They must also judge whether the sentence has been successfully completed.

5 If there is time, you may ask the groups to try another competition. Note that each competition will only take 5–10 minutes to answer.

---

11 *Language* Non-specific

Vocabulary Non-specific

Level Intermediate   *Time* 25–30 minutes

Material Crosswords with clues and their answers, usually published in the following day's newspaper

Preparation None

---

1 Form groups of two or three. Give each group a crossword with clues. Ask them to try and do as much of it as they can.

2 When they have finished, give each group the answers to their crosswords. Ask them to check how many answers were correct.

3 Give each group a different set of crossword answers. Ask them to write the clues in the style of the crossword completed in 1.

4 When everyone is ready, ask the groups to pass their crossword and clues to their neighbours who should then try and do as much of it as possible.

---

12 *Language* Non-specific

Vocabulary Non-specific

Level Intermediate +   *Time* 25–30 minutes

Material Tape recorder; a recording of the latest radio news; copies of the latest newspapers

Preparation The recording of the radio news should, if possible, be from the morning's news bulletin.

1 Form groups of four or five. Give each group a copy of the newspaper. Ask them to scan the front page and one or two other pages looking for the most important news items.

2 Explain that while the radio news will cover a number of different news items, it will usually only have three or four items of major interest which form the headlines for the bulletin. Ask each group to choose which four headlines are likely to be included in the bulletin. They should use the newspaper articles to write a sentence or two about these items. Ask them to try and include the most important facts.

3 When everyone is ready, play the recording of the radio news. Ask them to check if they have chosen the same items as the radio bulletin.

---

13 *Language* Making deductions; giving opinions; agreeing and disagreeing

Vocabulary Non-specific

Level Intermediate +   *Time* 15–20 minutes

Material Amusing misprints taken from magazines and newspapers; many publications print their own selection of misprints (e.g. *Punch, SHE, Private Eye* etc.). Here are some examples:

Martin Tyler, aged 33, of Greyhound Lane, Norton, admitted three charges of carless driving, failing to stop after and accident, and not reporting the accident.

Young budgies, all colours £3. Old Age Pensioners £2.

OLIVERS, Union Terrace. Ideal for pre- and after dinner meals, informal American-style diner.

Home life is the core of our civilization and is often the cause of crime among the young.

Be a Writer. Editors pay £000s for Short Stories and Articles.

Preparation Copy out the misprints onto cards.

---

1 Form groups of three or four. Give a misprint card to each group. Explain that the text is an extract from a newspaper or a magazine which includes either a misprint or a sentence which is ambiguous in its style, both creating an unintentionally humorous effect. Ask them to discover what the mistake is.

7

2 When they have found the mistake, they should rewrite the text.

3 More creative groups can use these extracts as the basis for amusing sketches, which can be prepared and performed for the rest of the class.

---

14 *Language* Non-specific

Vocabulary Non-specific

Level Intermediate +   *Time* 3 hours

Material A number of newspapers and magazines; a cassette recorder; microphone; cassette

Preparation None

---

1 Discuss with the students the different kinds of news to be found in a newspaper. Ask them to suggest a list of about eight or nine headings, e.g. home news, foreign news, business, the arts, TV guide, the weather, a profile of a politician or businessman, sport.

2 Form groups of three or four. Choose one group to act as editors. The other groups should choose one heading which interests them. The editors should make sure that, if possible, groups do not choose the same heading.

3 Give each group some newspapers. Ask them to look for four or five articles related to the heading they have chosen. Ask them to prepare a brief summary of them. The editors should visit all the groups in turn offering help and advice.

4 When the groups are ready, the editors should call a meeting. They must explain that they have to prepare a radio news bulletin lasting fifteen minutes. The bulletin must contain as large a variety of items as possible. The editions ask each group to give a summary of the articles they have chosen. They should then choose one or two items from each group and allot a proportion of the total programme time to them (usually one or two minutes). They must also remember that some time will be needed for introducing the bulletin, announcing the headlines, linking each item and closing remarks. The time given to each group's items should be marked on the board. The editors then explain that the bulletin will be broadcast in exactly one hour (or less), and that each group must have its items ready by then.

5 Each group then prepares its items and edits them to exactly the right length. It should try and involve as many of its members as possible in presenting the item.

6 The editors should check that each group is working towards the broadcasting schedule; they should also prepare short passages to introduce, link and close the items.

7 At the planned time, the bulletin is 'broadcast' and recorded.

3 Students usually like to hear the recording so you may like to use it to correct any mistakes.

Note that the broadcast time is obviously not essential, but it helps to create a sense of urgency and stops the activity from going over time.

Play on words
Word games

---

1 *Language* Making deductions

Vocabulary Non-specific

Level Elementary   *Time* 20–25 minutes

Material None

Preparation None
This is a version of 'Hangman' adapted for language learners.

---

1   Form groups of four or five. Ask one person in each group to think
    of a word of not less than seven letters, and then make the number
    of letters with a series of dashes. In turn, the other students say
    one letter each. If the letter is contained in the word, it is marked
    in its correct position above the dash. If the letter is not contained
    in the word, a line representing part of the gallows (see below) is
    drawn.

2   Each time a student guesses a letter which does not occur in the
    word, a further part is added to the gallows in the order marked
    below. There are ten parts to the gallows and if there are ten wrong
    guesses, the person who thought of the word wins a point.
    Note that in the example below, letters which occur twice have to
    be suggested twice. Where time is limited, letters which occur twice
    or more can all be marked at the same time.

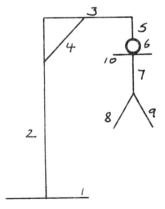

N A _ I O _ _ L _ T Y

(NATIONALITY)

2 *Language* Non-specific

Vocabulary The alphabet

Level Elementary   *Time* 20–25 minutes

Material A reading passage with the lines numbered

Preparation None

1 Ask each student to take a sheet of paper and to write down any twenty-five letters in a square five letters across and five down. Explain that the same letter may be repeated several times.

2 Ask a student to give you two numbers between 1 and 30, such as 17 and 10. Look at the text, find line 17 and letter 10 on this line and call it out. Explain that any students who have this letter on their sheets of paper should circle it. Write down the letters as you call them out.

3 Ask the next student to give you two more numbers. Continue as in 2.

4 The first student to have a horizontal, vertical or diagonal line of circled letters should show his/her paper to you. Check that the correct letters are circled. If they are correct, the student wins a point.

5 This game can also be played in groups of four or five. The students should take it in turns to be the one who calls out the letters.

3 *Language* Non-specific

Vocabulary Using the dictionary

Level Elementary +   *Time* 15–20 minutes

Material Cards; a class set of dictionaries

Preparation Choose about twenty words. Look up the word in the dictionary and write its definition on separate cards.

1 Form groups of three or four. Give each group a definition card. Ask them to use the dictionary to understand the definition and to find the word.

2 When they have done this successfully, give them another definition card. Continue as in 1.

3 The first group to find all twenty words is the winner.

4 *Language* Non-specific
Vocabulary Non-specific
Level Elementary   *Time* 5–10 minutes
Material None
Preparation None

---

1 Form groups of three or four. Ask them to name *one* type of tree. The group should confer quickly and one member should raise his/her hand. The first group to answer correctly wins a point.

2 Ask them to name *two* household pets, *three* types of meat, *four* rooms of the house, *five* farm animals, *six* parts of the car, *seven* pieces of furniture, *eight* parts of the body, *nine* things to eat, *ten* hobbies. The first group to answer each time gets a point.

3 The group with the highest number of points is the winner.

---

5 *Language* Making suggestions; agreeing and disagreeing
Vocabulary Non-specific
Level Elementary   *Time* 20–25 minutes
Material None
Preparation None

---

1 Explain that a time capsule with twenty everyday objects inside is going to be buried.

2 Form groups of five or six. Ask them to choose twenty everyday objects which represent our lives today. They should write their list down on a piece of paper.

3 Form new groups with one member from each of the old groups. Ask them to explain what they have decided to include in the time capsule and why. Encourage students to question the representative nature of each other's choice.

---

6 *Language* Describing use; making suggestions; agreeing and disagreeing
Vocabulary Non-specific
Level Elementary +   *Time* 20–25 minutes
Material Cards
Preparation Write on separate cards the following:
Art, Leisure, Work, Education, Housing, Holidays, Fashion, Communications, Transport, Science

---

1 Form groups of five or six. Explain that a time capsule is going to buried containing twenty objects which have great importance in our everyday lives. Give each group one card and ask them to choose *ten* objects related to the aspect of life written on it.

2 When everyone is ready, form new groups with one member from each of the old groups. Each student should explain his/her old group's choice of objects. The new group should then discuss which twenty objects they will include in the time capsule; they should try and include at least one object from all the aspects of life marked on the cards.

3 Half of each group should visit its neighbours. Ask them to imagine that two hundred years have passed. They have discovered the time capsule and want to know what the objects in the neighbouring group's list were used for. The host group should try to explain why the objects were representative of their time.

4 Ask students which everyday objects are likely to still exist in 100 years' time. Will they still be in exactly the same form? What are the most lasting discoveries of the twentieth century?

---

7 *Language* Giving definitions

Vocabulary Non-specific

Level Elementary +   *Time* 5–10 minutes

Material Cards

Preparation Write on separate cards each part of the following compounds:

hair cut	hand shake
match stick	out put
baby sitter	post box
book shelf	rain fall
bus stop	tax payer
door step	washing machine
ear ring	traffic light

Variation 1

1 Give each student a card. Ask them to go round the room saying their word until they meet another student with whom they can form a compound.

2 When they have found one partner, they should make a note of the compound and continue to look for others. After two or three minutes, check that the students have formed correct compounds.

3 Give the students another two or three minutes before checking again on the compounds they have formed.

Variation 2

1 For a more lively version, music can be played while the students go round saying their word. Stop the music suddenly from time to time. Ask them to find a definition for the compound they have formed with their temporary partner. Explain that it does not matter whether the compound formed is correct or not. For example, ring-shake – a toy for babies, baby machine – a device for rocking the baby to sleep.

3 Choose any pair and ask them to give their compound noun and its definition. With the rest of the class, decide if the definition sounds confused. If so, the pair must leave the game. If not, they may continue and you must ask other pairs for their compound noun and definition until you find one which is too confused for the pair to continue.

4 When the music stops the next time, the last pair to leave the game may ask any pair still playing to give their compound noun and definition. Continue as in 3.

5 The winners are the last pair still playing the game.

---

8 *Language* Non-specific

Vocabulary The alphabet

Level Elementary +   *Time* 15–20 minutes

Material Cards

Preparation Write on separate cards the following words:

resplendent	humiliation	regulation	bureaucracy
wholesome	federation	endowment	horsemanship
condominium	counterweight	inflationary	dictatorship

Form groups of three or four. Give each group a card. Ask them to find as many words of three or more letters using only the letters included in the word on the card.

---

9 *Language* Non-specific

Vocabulary The alphabet

Level Elementary +   *Time* 20–25 minutes

Material Cards or sheets of paper

Preparation None

---

1 Form pairs. Give each pair a large number of cards or ask them to cut or tear sheets of paper into card-size squares. Each person

should mark the letters of the alphabet on separate cards. Each pair will produce two sets of the alphabet.

2 Ask them to separate the vowels from the consonants.

3 Ask them to turn to their neighbours. The four sets of consonants and the four sets of vowels are placed in two piles.

4 Ask pair A to take nine letters, taking consonants or vowels as it wishes; explain that they are only allowed to take the letters from the top of the piles and are not allowed to choose the exact letter. With the nine letters, pair A has two minutes to find a word of at least three letters and using as many letters as possible. At the same time Pair B will also try to find a word using the same letters.

5 When the two minutes are over, each pairs will say how many letters are contained in the word they have made. The pair with the greater number of letters will say their word. If both sides agree that the word is correctly spelt, this pair wins as many points as it has letters in the word (e.g. seven letters, seven points).

6 Pair B should then continue as in 4.

7 The pair with the highest number of points at the end of three or four rounds is the winner.

---

10 *Language* Giving definitions

Vocabulary Non-specific

Level Intermediate   *Time* 15–20 minutes

Material Cards

Preparation Write on separate cards peculiar, little-used words such as *fester, scapegoat, jostle, spatter,* and nonsense words such as *bedcar, hospitalacious, grindling, scaggle.*

---

1 Form groups of three or four. Give each group a card. Ask them to decide whether the word is a real one or a nonsense one.

2 Ask them to write a possible definition for the word.

3 When they have finished they should pass their word to their neighbour and receive one in exchange. Continue as in 1 and 2.

4 When each group has seen and written definitions for all the words, hold up each card and ask the groups a) if they think the word is real or not and b) to give their definitions.

5 Explain which words are real and give their definitions.

11 *Language* Non-specific

Vocabulary Non-specific

Level Intermediate   *Time* 10–15 minutes

Material Cards

Preparation Write on separate cards each word of a number of well-known proverbs, e.g.:
Don't put all your eggs in one basket.
Every cloud has a silver lining.
A stitch in time saves nine.
A rolling stone gathers no moss.
You can't have your cake and eat it.
Where there's a will, there's a way.
Make hay while the sun shines.
Necessity is the mother of invention.

1 Shuffle the cards and spread them around the room. Explain that the words all make up eight different proverbs. Ask them to try and reconstruct the proverbs.

2 If they have found the correct proverbs, ask them to consider whether there is an equivalent proverb in their own language. Ask them to try and translate it word for word into English.

3 If, as is likely, they do not know the proverbs, ask them to make up nonsense proverbs using the words on the cards e.g. Don't eat eggs while your mother has cake. Make sure that they create proverbs which are more or less grammatically correct.

4 When everyone has finished, reconstruct the correct proverbs and discuss with the group what they mean.

5 Form groups of three or four. Ask each group to choose a proverb without letting the other groups know which they have chosen. Ask them to prepare a short mime sketch which illustrates the proverb.

6 When everyone is ready, ask each group to perform its mime sketch. The others should try and guess which proverb is being illustrated.

12 *Language* Giving definitions

Vocabulary Non-specific

Level Intermediate   *Time* 45–60 minutes

Material Cards

Preparation Write on one side of separate cards a word which the students are unlikely to know. Here are some examples:

Eavesdrop	Liverpudlian
Anglepoise	Wistful
Curfew	Knuckle
Picaroon	Chisel
Kipper	Elevenses

On the reverse side write a short dictionary explanation:

e.g. *Eavesdrop* – to listen to a private conversation

Anglepoise – an adjustable reading lamp

Curfew – a period usually during the night when people are not allowed out of their homes.

There should be about one card for three people.

This is a version of the television game 'Call my Bluff'.

1 This is a complicated game and it is a good idea to perform a sample round with the help of two of the better students whom you will have briefed beforehand.

2 Explain that the students will hear three definitions of the same word; two of these definitions are false, one is true. They must decide which is the true definition.

3 Show them the word e.g. Eavesdrop and give your definition:
'Eavesdrop comes from the Old English and refers to the part of the house where the roof overhangs the walls, or where the "eaves drop". In olden days, this was where spies used to stand when they wanted to discover what plans their enemies were making, or to listen to the secret conversations taking place inside the house. So, these days, the verb "to eavesdrop" means to overhear a private conversation.'

Note that the story leading to the true definition does not have to be strictly accurate.

Then ask one of your helpers to give another definition;
'Eavesdrop refers to that time of day when night falls and tomorrow comes closer. "Eve" is often used in English to mean the day before an important day such as Christmas Eve, New Year's Eve. The word brings to mind a nice, cosy feeling, blazing log fire, warm slippers and a faithful dog with its head on your lap. "Eavesdrop" means the early evening.'

Then ask for the last definition:
'Eavesdrop comes from the Saxon word "Effe" which means to hover, and the Old English word "droppe" which means to drop. The word refers to the last drop which comes from a bottle, which hovers and drops into your glass. As we all know, the person who finishes the bottle will be lucky enough to get married or to have a baby within the year to come. So, to wish someone "Eavesdrop" is to wish them good luck in the future.'

4 Give a quick summary of the definitions and then ask the other students to vote for what they think is the correct definition. The definition with the greatest number of votes will then be revealed

91

to be true or false. If it is false, the students can vote for the remaining definitions.

5 Form groups of three (with one or two groups of four, if necessary). Give each group a card with a word and its definition. Explain that they must prepare two false definitions and elaborate the real one so that all three are in the same style. Give each group about ten to fifteen minutes to prepare their definitions. Make sure that they cannot be overheard by other groups. You should pass from group to group giving help and making suggestions if necessary.

6 When everyone is ready, ask each group to give their word and definitions to the rest of the class. Continue as in 4.

---

13 *Language* Non-specific

Vocabulary The alphabet

Level Intermediate   *Time* 25–30 minutes

Material Cards

Preparation Write a number of four-letter words on separate cards. If necessary, these can be prepared by the students themselves.
This is a version of the game 'Mastermind' played with letters.

---

1 Form pairs. Explain that Student A in each pair will be given a word which he must not show to the other. Student B must try and guess what the word is.

2 To do this, student B writes down any four letter word. If it contains a letter in student A's word, A marks a circle beside the word. If B has guessed a correct letter in the correct place, A marks a circle with a cross in it. For every wrong letter in the word. A marks a dot.
Note that the position of these circles, crosses and dots should not correspond to the position of the letters in the word (see example below).

2 B then guesses another four-letter word using the information gathered with his/her first guess to try and discover which letter(s) was/were in the correct position. This should continue until B has discovered A's word.

Example:

A's word: SINK

B writes: 1 BIRD   A writes: ⊕ :
                                     ·

            2 BACK   ⊕ ⊕
                                    · ·

            3 BOLD   ⊕ :
                                    ·

            4 SOLD   ⊕ :
                                    ·

            5 SAND   ⊕ ⊕
                                    · ·

            etc.

Indexes

Language

Vocabulary

The *alphabet*   8.2, 8.8, 8.9, 8.13
Physical *appearance*   Role card
   activity, 1.2, 1.4, 1.6
Clothing   Role card activity, 1.2, 1.4,
   1.6
Adjectives of *critical opinion*   4.9, 7.9
Adjectives of *colour*   2.2
Countries   6.2, 6.3, 6.11
Dates   2.11
Emotions   1.4
Films   4.2
Food   4.7, 4.8
Furniture   3.6, 3.10
Geographical description   6.1, 6.4, 6.6,
   6.9
Parts of the *house*   3.3, 3.5, 3.6, 3.9,
   3.10
Household items   3.1, 3.2
Housing   Role card activity
Intellectual activities   2.11
Jobs   2.3, 2.4, 2.6, 2.10, 2.12

Leisure activities   4.1, 4.13
Adjectives of material   2.2, 2.5, 3.2, 3.9
Money   5.8
Nationalities   6.3
Numbers   4.7
Personal and professional qualities   2.12
Politics   7.7
Prepositions   3.3, 3.5, 3.6, 3.7, 6.5
Shops   5.1
Shopping items   5.1, 5.7, 5.11, 5.13
Adjectives of size and shape   2.1, 2.5,
   3.2, 3.4, 3.5, 3.9
Sports   4.3
Sports equipment   4.3
Tools   2.1, 2.6
Tourist facilities   6.5, 6.8
Town facilities   3.8, 3.11
Parts of the *town*   6.2, 6.6, 6.7
TV programmes   7.9
Places of *work*   2.10